My Four Lives

Memoirs of a Singing Psychoanalyst

To Prof. Harry Zohn
with sincere thanks for your
encouragement

12/11/99

Manfred Hecht

My Four Lives
Memoirs of a Singing Psychoanalyst

ARIADNE PRESS
Riverside, California

Library of Congress Cataloging-in-Publication Data

Hecht, Manfred
    My four lives : memoirs of a singing psychoanalyst /
Manfred Hecht
            p.   cm. -- (Biography, autobiography, memoirs series)
        ISBN 1-57241-085-X
        1. Hecht, Manfred. 2. Psychoanalysts--United States Biography.
    3. Singers--United States. I. Title. II. Series: Studies in Austrian literature,
    culture, and thought. Biography, autobiography, memoirs series.
    RC438.6.H43A3 1999
    616.89'17'092--dc21
    [B]   99-15169
                                                              CIP

Cover Design:
Kurt Collins
Photo: Courtesy Norman Handelmann

This book is dedicated to the memory of my parents, Ada and Maximilian Hecht, both innocent victims of one of history's most evil crimes.

Acknowledgments

Sincere thanks to Janice Booker for her editorial suggestions, help and encouragement, to Dr. Desmond R. Tivy for his editorial proofreading help, and to my partner for many years, Marie, without whose inspiration and patience this book would never have happened. My appreciation also to Barbara Wind Morcheles and my friend, Dr. Frank Lachmann, for their helpful comments. I am grateful to Henry Gelfand for his technical help with computer problems.

I — DAYS OF WRATH

March is still cold and damp in Austria with no hint of the lurking spring. It was like that the night of March 12, 1938, as a friend and I left the theater in Vienna. I shivered slightly and drew my scarf tighter around my neck. As I pulled my gloves out of my pocket, I saw him. I had not expected to meet my father who stood at the entrance to the theater. He looked very pale, ill at ease, and motioned us urgently towards a waiting taxi. As we came closer, he hugged me for a short moment and whispered for us to be silent.

Once we were in the cab, he told us that the Austrian government had resigned, that the German army was marching into Austria at this very moment, and that, in the absence of any existing authority, mobs were roaming the streets. Glancing out the taxi window I experienced a surge of intense fear as I watched menacing groups of men, as if emerging from the gutters, gathering together.

We managed to deliver my friend to her family in the suburbs and raced home. It was time to acknowledge that the end had come, and that we had to make immediate plans if there was going to be any hope for survival. When my parents and I thought of survival then, we thought about building a new life, or at least of creating an illusion of security in our present existence. Even at this late time, we could not believe that the political changes we were experiencing would actually end up in mass murder, or that very soon survival would literally mean escaping death. After all, we reasoned, the Germans were civilized people, they had produced and nurtured great philosophers, scientists, musicians, writers; in the midst of their current obsession with the Nazis, the Germans might become temporary oppressors, might drive out the Jews, but surely they would not exterminate us.

The next day a crowd of almost a million Viennese gathered on the Heldenplatz to welcome, cheer and adore the Führer. That night I wrote to everybody I could think of who lived abroad, to explore any possibility to flee my country.

And so began six months of extreme stress, tension, and tragedy. The unthinkable had become the reality. All the attempts to look away, to pretend it was not so, to find rational sounding solutions were over. The man who had vowed to destroy me and mine had come to power and his army and his followers were taking control of our lives. Hopes were gone that the Western Powers, or the Czechs, or the Italians, would not let it happen. Hitler and his hordes took over and murdered the Austria I had known while the world stood by.

Just as a dying person often experiences an upsurge of well-being shortly before the end comes, the existing government of Austria, sensing that its days were numbered, facing a German military ultimatum, aware that it could not count on outside intervention, and recognizing the absence of popular support, gambled. The Chancellor announced that free elections would be held within a very short time and lifted all political restrictions on the parties who wished to campaign.

For three short days before the Anschluss, we citizens were allowed to inhale the delicious perfume of democracy. With a large number of other students, I found myself climbing on one of the many trucks that suddenly became available. Flags, posters and pamphlets were on board, exhorting people to vote for the Social Democratic Party, the "party of unity." In case of attack, there was even a supply of night sticks stashed away so we would not be defenseless. All this was supplied by the underground of the party which had been outlawed until then.

Feverish with excitement and a youthful sense of power we rode throughout the city of Vienna and the suburbs, waving flags, shouting "Freedom!" We distributed pamphlets, sang forbidden songs, and thrilled to the welcoming response we received, especially in the workers' districts. But that exuberance was quickly over.

I realized very soon that all police authority had been trans-ferred to roaming gangs who either wore brown shirts or just arm bands with a swastika; some had rifles. Anybody not wearing a swastika button was presumed to be Jewish and fair game. A foreign passport or a passing officer of the German Army who might sometimes intervene were the only protection against any imaginable outrage. These gangs would "arrest" their victims randomly, so that any time I ventured out, I risked detention.

Some of those arrested disappeared forever; some ended up in concentration camps or in Gestapo cellars; others just escaped with a beating or some other humiliation. Personal property, cars, businesses, could be "confiscated," simply by handing the owner a slip of paper with a scribbled signature, while a partner trained his weapon on the victim.

I was "arrested" twice. The first time I was walking with a colleague from medical school to discuss possible future plans when we were stopped by a patrol. I was released after being ordered to clean some soiled toilets. While carrying out my assignment I did my best to entertain my captors with the most gruesome details of my medical dissections in the hope that I might cause them some queasiness and nausea. In retrospect these displays of youthful bravado seem quite frivolous when held against the tragedies that were to come.

I soon learned to walk through the streets with my left arm held across my chest, attempting to hide the area of my lapel where my fellow citizens wore their swastika insignias. For me to wear one of those was not only morally indefensible, but also entailed serious risks in case of an identity check. Soon after I left Austria, all Jews were ordered to wear the Star of David, making it easier to find the hunted prey, but I did not have to cope with that complication.

The danger of random arrests was not limited to the streets. Small groups of "brownshirts" would roam through various neighborhoods and ascertain from the buildings' superintendents whether any Jews were living in the house. Thus I was "arrested" a second time. Again, I was fortunate to be released, although the gall and sheer nerve afforded to the young, helped.

I came home one day, not too long after the takeover, and found my father in a high state of excitement. Two storm troopers had come and asked for me and announced that they would return. As an example of our naivete, my father decided that we would go to the local police precinct and ask for protection. On the way, we were stopped by two brownshirts, but my father's display of a document certifying that he had received a decoration for rendering services to Austria got us out of that jam.

Once we arrived at the police station, it became clear that the police were not interested, citing "jurisdictions, policies, etc." and would just ignore the complaint. That night I called the father of a friend, an American who represented the U.S. treasury in Austria, and told him of my predicament. He was most sympathetic, promised to include the information in his official report to Washington, but could offer no assistance. There was no place for me to go or hide. So my parents and I decided I would have to take my chances.

The next morning, bright and early, the two storm troopers showed up to take me away. It so happened, by a fluke, that my draft call to the Austrian army had fallen on a date after the German Army had taken over, and bureaucratic red tape had not caught up with the rush of developments. I had appeared before the draft board as required, was assigned to a reserve unit, and routinely granted a deferment pending completion of my medical studies. The document was signed and stamped with the seal of the German Army Command which included the swastika emblem.

The "arresting" storm troopers covering the area where I lived had learned from the superintendent that a young Jewish man lived in the house. They brought me to their local headquarters, a former Jewish athletic club, Maccabi, to which I had once belonged. There they presented me to their superior, a young man with some emblems on his brown shirt. He curtly ordered me to undress. Unbelievable as this seems to me now, I responded by cautioning him that I was a member of the German Armed Forces, produced my draft deferment, and suggested that he check with the German Army High Command before proceeding any further, so that both of us might be spared some trouble. He hesitated for a moment and let me go.

The next months, preceding my eventual escape in August of that year, were probably among the most agonizing and painful of my life up to this very day. The anguish slowly built to a nadir, when on my way to a new life and freedom, I had to say goodbye to those I loved and leave them to their fate. Even now, as I write this, I can feel my resistance to the reopening of old wounds, and my heart pounds as I hesitate to go on.

It was not the danger to life and limb, nor the imposed humiliations that were hardest to bear. Rather, it was the helplessness and uncertainty, the sense of betrayal by long time neighbors, the awareness that the most favorable possible outcome would entail separation from, and abandonment of, my parents, my family and friends.

An example of the existing climate: the local party chief, the "Gauleiter," ordered that on a particular day no food would be sold or given to Jews. So, for just one day this time, the grocers, butchers, and bakers who had done business with my family for so many years, refused to deal with us.

In those days the official policy was still aimed at harassing Jews so that they would depart; it was only later that direct efforts began to exterminate them. As another display of petty meanness, the University would only certify that I had completed part of my medical studies if I signed an affidavit vowing never again to return. I was moved to see tears in the eyes of the young woman clerk who gave me the documents and filed my statement.

My greatest difficulty was not the matter of escape which, with a little bit of luck and patience, could possibly be managed. The real problem was to find a country that would admit this refugee. All borders were closed, and only considerable funds available abroad could help provide temporary asylum. The only real hope for salvation was an immigration visa to the United States.

Thousands of people stood in line from dawn to dusk at the American Consulate, just to receive a number that would register them for an application if all the other requirements could be satisfied. There they stood, in constant fear that a storm trooper patrol would use the opportunity to round up Jews.

To qualify for the magic visa, two main conditions had to be met. First, an American citizen had to sign an affidavit and complete the necessary papers to guarantee that the prospective immigrant would not become a burden to the United States. Second, an immigration quota number would have to become available. These quotas had been set by law, based on the number of immigrants from various regions during one given year in the twenties. Your nationality at the time of birth determined what quota you belonged to. As I was born in Vienna, and not too many Austrians had immigrated to the U.S., a quota number was obtainable in a relatively short time.

This was not true for my parents, as my father was born in the prewar Austrian part of Poland, and my mother in the prewar Russian part of Poland. Therefore, they were counted under these respective country quotas which were filled for years to come. With many others, they were murdered because the American authorities enforced the quota system harshly and inflexibly.

My friend's father, the member of the American Diplomatic Service, gave me hope that a visa application would be expedited if I could provide the coveted affidavit signed by an American citizen. The only person I knew in the States was Alice, a former girlfriend. She had moved to New York about a year earlier and was living with relatives. With the help of her uncle, kind strangers in New York signed an affidavit for me. There was an explicit understanding that I would not, under any circumstances, burden them or the United States authorities with my upkeep.

After endless standing in various lines, surviving innumerable frustrations and bureaucratic obstacles connected with obtaining emigration and immigration papers, I finally possessed that cherished document, a U.S. Visa and Green Card. The card promised that the bearer could eventually apply for citizenship and was permitted to work.

In the midst of all this turmoil, the routine of life went on. I ate, slept, even played, studied English shorthand and typing, and as best as I could, ignored the horrors that were happening around me as well as the prospect that much worse was to come.

Even then, we knew that from moment to moment our immediate survival was at risk. It was open season on Jews, and at any given time the authorities or any overenthusiastic squad leader could do away with one or all of us. So subtle was the threat, so powerful the enemy, and so strong the need to believe in one's chances for survival, that in contrast to the later situation in the Warsaw Ghetto there was not, and could not reasonably be, any thought of active resistance.

Frantic preparations for my trip to the States absorbed most of my energy and attention. It was then possible to purchase a boat ticket on an Italian or German ship with Austrian currency. The emigrant was allowed personal property and a maximum of the equivalent of four U.S. dollars. To be caught with more money while crossing the border could mean the risk of severe punishment, possibly death.

My parents used their savings to outfit me with as many tailor-made suits as I could manage to carry. I believe there were seventeen. They also purchased lots of shirts, shoes and other articles of clothing. To make it possible for me to survive in an emergency, my father gave me some valuable personal possessions: a gold cigarette case, a keepsake from a very close friend, a gold precision pocket watch, and a diamond and pearl tie clasp. I still have these cherished objects. Comfortable accommodations on the Italian ocean liner S.S."Rex" were arranged. For all we knew, the days on board ship would, for the foreseeable future, provide my only opportunity to eat adequately or to sleep under a safe roof.

My father collected seventy letters of recommendation. Some came from a friend of his, the Vienna correspondent of *The New York Times*, and included introductions to the family of the publisher and to other highly placed individuals of his acquaintance.

Another general letter of reference and recommendation came from His Majesty, Ferdinand, King of Bulgaria, to whom my father had been of service in a business matter at one time. Everything that could be done to ease the plunge into uncertainty was done.

Over all the preparations, the hopes for survival, even the excitement of the impending challenges and adventures, hung a heavy cloud of almost unbearable sadness. The anticipation of separating from, and, in fact, abandoning my parents and friends to an unpredictable and perilous fate outweighed all the threats of immediate mortal risks. The Greeks referred to heavy emotions as being felt in the diaphragm, (eni tymo); I felt then as if I were to blow up from the accumulated pressure of my anguish, and I feel some of that now as I remember.

Surrounded by a wall of meanness and hostility, I deeply appreciated some instances of kindness, compassion, and even courage displayed by a few non-Jews during that time. I mentioned the tears in the eyes of the woman clerk at the university who issued my certificate of leave in exchange for my signed declaration that I would never again return to study there. My old friend, Erika, by then on her way to becoming a well-known actress, insisted on a farewell meeting at considerable risk to her career and, quite possibly, to herself. There are warm memories of those, some even strangers, who did not speak out but whose eyes conveyed their embarrassment and impotent guilt.

August tenth, 1938, arrived: the day of my departure for Trieste, Italy, where I was to board my ship. I was on the threshold of a new life: survival, opportunities, adventure were beckoning to me. And yet, it was a day of the most unforgettable agony I have ever known. No matter how often I allowed myself, even forced myself, to relive with uncontrollable tears the scene of my departure during my own psychoanalysis, the memory continues to hurt as much as ever, even more than half a century later. The imprinted images persist with grievous clarity.

I am standing at the window of the express train that was to take me away. In my pockets, I finger my father's treasured possessions, a last insurance against extreme need. On the platform stand my parents, my father desperately trying not to show his tears and to maintain a measure of control; my mother looking at me with such pain in her eyes as I have never seen before or ever after. It is the saddest moment of my life, burned unforgettably and forever into my brains and guts. As the train slowly pulls out, I have a moment of foreboding that this was the last time, that we would never see each other again. And so it was to be.

As I write this, a seemingly maudlin musical memory comes into my head. It is an aria from Puccini's *Madama Butterfly* that I had so often heard my mother sing and rehearse. The beauty of her voice and the music had sometimes reduced me to tears in those happier days of my childhood. Mme. Butterfly is taking leave of her small child, Hope, who is about to depart with his father, Lieutenant Pinkerton; moments later Butterfly will commit suicide by *hara kari*. She is holding the child's head and imploring him to look at her, and to remember her face, the face of his mother.

After a surprisingly uneventful border crossing into Italy, with only a perfunctory examination by S.S. border police, I continued on to Trieste. I tipped the Austrian conductor who was returning to Vienna, and asked him to call my parents and tell them that I had crossed the border alive. He did. I checked into an inexpensive prepaid hotel and slept for fifteen hours. The next morning seemed very bright as, warmed by the Italian sun, I embarked on the promise, and the dread of a new life.

II — "VIENNA, CITY OF MY DREAMS..."

My crossing to America gave me ample time to reflect on the history, both global and personal, that brought me to this ship.

Three weeks after the armistice that ended the First ` World War, Vienna, where I was born, bore little resemblance to the romantic city of waltzes and songs. Millions had been killed in the war; many more maimed. When the borders of Europe were redrawn, Austria, on the losing side, was no longer an empire of more than forty million people, but a small country of six million. More than two million were starving in Vienna, the formerly glamorous capital of the Habsburgs.

My father spent the war representing a large Austrian bank and its war loan efforts in Yugoslavia and Poland. In Warsaw, he met and fell in love with my mother, then a young, very beautiful aspiring operatic soprano, nineteen years his junior. She had just completed postgraduate studies at the conservatory. They were married and soon moved to Vienna where my father's family had settled some time before.

I was born after the war into a city of many contradictions that were reflected in the cultural, political and economic forces that would affect me and my family over the next twenty years. The city administration was composed of liberal Social Democrats who established a progressive elementary school system, built model municipal housing for workers, and embraced high social goals.

The city government was backed by an artistic and intellectual elite, the leftovers from the explosion of creativity that had started at the end of the nineteenth century, the "Fin de Siècle" era, and had continued up to the First World War. In the last gasp of liberalism before the upsurge of nationalism had sent it into decline, Vienna had been the cultural focus of Europe. That time had passed. Yet, the echoes of Gustav Mahler, Richard Strauss, and Alban Berg could be heard amid the deprivations; the paintings of Klimt and Schiele, the creations of the Secession and the Bauhaus, now freed from the restraints of the more conservative monarchy, were approachable; the spirit of Freud, Schnitzler and Werfel still vitalized the intellectual community. Opera and theater flowered. The medical and scientific world of Vienna, against all financial odds, continued the fight to uphold a reputation for grand breakthroughs.

Still, despite some rebirth, the seeds of a coming catastrophe were there to be seen by those who cared to notice. Perhaps we knew that we were experiencing the dying gasps of an era, but we were able to deny that knowledge, and we continued to dance on top of the volcano until it erupted and blew us and itself to pieces.

As an infant I was not exposed to undue suffering. Through some friends, my parents were able to obtain condensed milk from United States Food Relief shipments so that I was adequately fed despite food shortages.

My parents both had their roots in different parts of Poland. My father was born in the Austrian part. His father, as I recall from family reminiscences, ran a mill, and/or a saloon. In any case, he sent his children, at least the boys, away to college. My father earned his "Matura," the equivalent of a college degree, in Prague, and went on to work for one of Austria's largest banks, the Wiener Bankverein. Through promotions he became the director of a branch right in the middle of Vienna, next to the Cathedral of St. Stephen.

He loved his work which provided a comfortable living, although clouds of financial worries, probably increased by concerns about extended family responsibilities were always present. We lived the typical upper middle class life of a somewhat assimilated Viennese-Jewish family of that time. We had a comfortable, large, well appointed and situated apartment, domestic help, and enjoyed the generous artistic, culinary, educational and cultural opportunities that Vienna still offered. Somehow, the available financial resources barely stretched enough to permit our lifestyle. Even before the catastrophic final period, there was some sense of living on the brink of disaster.

Father was a large, handsome, distinguished looking man who had become bald early in life. He was very easygoing, benign, and probably the most good natured and generous person I have ever known. For long periods, and at great personal sacrifice, he helped support his parents, his sister's family and various other relatives when they were in need.

I loved him very much, and I know that I was the apple of his eye. He was always very available to me, his only child. Viennese routine permitted him to come home for lunch, the main meal of the day, which we always ate together. Until adolescence, when my friends became so important to me, we spent a lot of time together taking long walks, on Sunday outings and vacations. Often, a friend and I would meet my father at his office, and we would walk home together.

He loved to tell funny stories. Even today I trace my pleasure in hearing and telling jokes to the delight of listening and laughing with him. It never occurred to me to follow him into banking. After my childhood wishes to become a butcher, baker and chef so that I could eat all the food I had prepared, there was never a doubt in my mind that my career would be in music or medicine.

I remember mother as a slender, blonde, blue-eyed woman, very attractive, with a beautiful soprano voice. She was less easygoing and more quick tempered than father. Born in the Russian part of prewar Poland, she had lost her father to pneumonia at a very early age. Her own mother had supported her three children by operating a printing business. Both my parents were convinced of the value of education and were willing to make sacrifices to provide the best for me. Mother, just because she was the parent more often at home, became the disciplinarian. She made sure that I did my homework, practiced the piano, and completed the French and English assignments for my tutors. My English teacher, Mrs. Leverton-Wetterschneider, an English woman who had married an Austrian, had to be satisfied with my preparations. Mother was policing my study habits, which were, at times, sluggish. This, I am sure, was not an easy task and led to some memorable confrontations. Fortunately for me, she tended to win most of them. Throughout, I felt her love, but I had an easier time with my father. None of us could have foreseen then that my facility with languages and my background in music, may have many years later, if not saved my life, eased my survival considerably. This discipline to study proved most helpful when I prepared operatic roles or completed my doctoral dissertation.

It was not until much more recently, in the course of my own analysis, that I was able to appreciate the powerful conflicting pressures mother must have had to struggle with when she dedicated herself to motherhood at the sacrifice of a promising career. She limited her opportunities as an opera singer by refusing all out of town engagements, and I remember overhearing many discussions of the offers she received. By restricting her performances to Vienna and accepting only a few brief guest appearances abroad, she foreclosed opportunities to become internationally recognized. Most of her creative energies were centered on myself, her only child. I suspect that she paid a heavy price of severe frustrations; this may have been related to the periods of fatigue, the lack of appetite, the weight loss: all the things that I remember well and today would see as signs of depression.

It is much easier to think back to the music which was always a part of our life. I was permitted to listen when mama studied her operatic parts with some world famous conductors who graciously tolerated my presence. So long as I was quiet, I could sit on the floor under the grand piano and listen. At parties, when there were musicales by mother and her colleagues, I was permitted to watch quietly. Later, as my skills at the piano grew, I was able, with some pride, to accompany mother. My knowledge of operatic and art-song repertoire as well as my love for music increased as I grew, as did my admiration for my mother's talent. Papa was very proud of mother's artistic successes and did all he could to help her.

Once, when mama was particularly nervous about a radio concert, papa conceived of a plot to help her out. In Austria, there was a well established superstition concerning chimney sweeps who were not seen very often on Vienna's streets. To meet a chimney sweep, black with coal dust, carrying all his paraphernalia, was considered good luck. On this occasion, papa somehow managed to find two chimney sweeps, and with the help of a small financial consideration, persuaded them to stand at the entrance to the radio studios. While he and I hid in a doorway, we watched mother arrive in a taxi, saw her face light up when she noticed them, and she entered the studio with a new bounce to her step.

The first opera performance I remember attending, when I was about seven, was Verdi's *Masked Ball*; mama sang the leading soprano role of Amelia. It was a great success, and made a lasting impression on me. I was often told the story of when my parents had taken me to the Vienna State Opera to see *Haensel and Gretl* when I was about five. This time mama was not in the cast, but in the box with me. When the witch made her entrance on stage, I began screaming at the top of my voice in apparent terror, and had to be removed hurriedly. (No wonder I cannot remember it.) Anyway, it became an often repeated family joke that the penetrating volume of my voice held great promise for a distinguished operatic career. Similar ear piercing exits, I was told, had been staged by me from various elegant dining rooms when, during vacations, my parents were bold enough to take me along.

My parents loved each other very much and provided me with a warm, protective and affectionate home. Their only quarrels occurred on rare occasions when papa yielded to the entreaties of his family and even went into debt in order to bail out some of his relatives. Mama had not quite forgiven them for having treated her as an intruder into the closely knit family when papa had first brought her home as his bride. Also, understandably, she minded having to pawn her jewelry in order to keep somebody whom she did not even like out of jail.

These early years provided me with ease and comfort and gave me the self-confidence which helped me to weather the stresses that were ahead. The years I attended elementary school were stimulating and enjoyable; there were good close friends, and life seemed wonderful to this young boy.

I was too young to realize what was happening in the world outside my protected life. Cut off from the support of the multi-ethnic Austrian empire, deprived of the Czech, Hungarian, Slavic and Italian creative cultural input, Vienna began to decline. The echoes of the golden age, the trailblazing cosmopolitan humanism that had blossomed around the preceding generation could still be heard; but they were echoes and they were dying. In the absence of adequate financial support, the center of artistic, scientific and intellectual progress moved away, mostly towards Berlin. Fed and spurred on by poverty and unemployment, anti-intellectualism, anti-Semitism, and nationalism gained ground quickly, and invaded the life of the city.

In the first nineteen years of my life I lived through three bloody uprisings that were crushed by government forces with considerable loss of life. The fourth one succeeded with the help of invading troops and ended the world I knew.

On July 15, 1927, I was returning from a swimming outing with mother's brother, a leading tenor at the Bremen Opera who was visiting us, when the streets reverberated with calls of vendors hawking extra editions of all newspapers. A large outpouring of Social Democratic workers had marched in protest against a court verdict. When they reached the Palace of Justice, not very far from my home, they set fire to it. The police opened fire on the demonstrators and more than a hundred of them died, with many more wounded. The distant sound of machine gun fire rang in my ears while the anxiety of the adults close to me provoked fear and fascination.

Seven years later, in February 1934, the conservative government ordered the army to open artillery fire on the workers' housing developments to suppress a general strike by the Social Democrats. My friends and I picked up discarded cartridge cases and watched the troops and police rush to the places of action. That same year, while on a student exchange in France, I learned that a Nazi plot had been quashed by armed force, and that the chancellor of Austria had been murdered by the plotters. By 1938, millions of

Austrians were enthusiastically welcoming Hitler and the invading German Army, and the Austrian government finally collapsed. The chancellor, Mr. Schuschnigg, resigned with a moving speech, the radio played Haydn's string quartet based on the old anthem, and that was that.

Prior to these years, as adolescence and puberty approached, the climate of strife and conflict increasingly affected me. At the same time, the transition from the warm, accepting climate of the progressive elementary school I had attended to the traditional, somewhat authoritarian environment of the gymnasium created its share of tensions.

In the Austrian educational system, children were assigned to separate types of schools after the first four years. Those who aspired to university studies and were found to qualify intellectually, the "academicians," went to various categories of middle schools, or "gymnasia," leading to the "Matura," the approximate equivalent of an American college degree. The "gymnasium" represented the European compromise of academic high school and college and prepared its graduates to enter university (medical school, law school, etc.) The other children finished their education in another class of schools with a four-year curriculum. All the middle schools were under control of the national conservative government and were run accordingly. I applied and was accepted by a "humanistic" gymnasium not far from my home, one that emphasized the study of Greek and Latin, Philosophy and Humanities.

My school, the "Wasagymnasium," had a reputation for strictness and achievement. Coming from a school where all classes were taught by the same warm and friendly teacher, the change to a classroom structure with different "professors" for each subject, daily quizzes, and strict discipline, was quite a shock for me.

Forty-five years later, when, as a visitor, I walked into the entrance hall, the "aula" of the Wasagymnasium, I was overwhelmed by the familiar scent of institutional disinfectant and sweating children, and re-experienced the nervousness and excitement of my ten-year-old self reporting for his entrance exam.

Our class was coeducational (there were two girls), and as we represented the offspring of a war generation, there were only a few of us. All professors were men with advanced degrees. Although we learned a lot, we also hated school fervently and viewed our courses as something we had to endure and complete as ably and quickly as possible. We questioned what the extended courses in ancient languages would mean to our future, but we learned to approach our tasks pragmatically and to avoid problems and obstacles. Looking back, and with mixed feelings, I appreciate the exposure to knowledge in diverse fields, and to a disciplinary system that, for better or worse, insisted that students pass their exams and did not encourage questions about relevance. During my later graduate studies this austere training helped me complete my program in record time, while my colleagues struggled with conflicts about yielding to the system.

In addition to school, I had piano lessons and private lessons in English and French. At sixteen, I was accepted at the State Academy of Music, and continued piano and composition there. When my voice had fully changed, voice lessons were added to my schedule.

As I write this, it feels to me as if there could not have been enough time to breathe, eat or sleep. Yet, I know that I did find ample time to play, hike, read, listen to music and date. How my friends and I were able to do all this, I can no longer explain, but somehow we managed.

Early adolescence was as difficult and significant for me as it is for all teenagers. I was a fat child. In previous years that had not mattered too much; now with increased emphasis on athletic activities, I was painfully aware of my physical clumsiness. Although among the tallest in my class, I was also among the heaviest.

Any unhappiness I experienced at this time was heightened by Herr Professor Wagner. Between my tenth and thirteenth year, he became the bane of my existence. A swarthy, slim and athletic man in his early thirties, he was in overall charge of my class. He also taught history, geography, and supervised all athletic activities.

Professor Wagner was an interesting history teacher who could muster up enough charisma to make a profound impression on his students and instill some personal admiration for himself; this was especially true when he presented historical events that related to patriotism, nationalism and the importance of a greater Germany that would absorb Austria and would include it as its Eastern province, the Ostmark. His voice, at these declarations, became emotion-charged and dramatic, seducing his young audience.

Herr Professor Wagner was not only a fanatical Nazi and anti-Semite, he was also pathologically sadistic. He needed a scapegoat among his students on whom he could concentrate as much scorn, mockery and abuse as possible. He then attempted to direct the hostility and contempt of the other children towards his target, trying to break down his victim psychologically and physically.

As I was Jewish, fat, and not conspicuously stupid, I became Herr Professor Wagner's chosen challenge. For me, he became the model for all the Gestapo villains portrayed in Hollywood movies during World War II. For three years he abused me without mercy, mocked me, made me the physical target of hardball practice during the gym periods, quizzed me during each class period, carefully choosing areas that had not been covered and which I could not answer. His cruelty became so obvious that even this group of young adolescents rallied to my support rather than participate in his campaign to degrade me.

After the initial shock of this treatment wore off, there was a period during which I was just a very unhappy child who dreaded to wake up every morning to face another ordeal in Wagner's classes. I felt systematically humiliated, helplessly caught in a trap that I could not escape no matter how hard I tried. Even after the rest of my classmates stopped laughing at the jokes the professor made at my expense, it still remained a contest between a powerful authority figure and a little boy of twelve, already struggling with adolescence. When I attempted to discuss the situation with my parents, they were empathic, but, in the spirit of the times, gave the benefit of doubt to the Herr Professor. I agonized for a long time and arrived at a conscious plan of action. I knew that I had no way of confronting my torturer openly; I decided that I would think of myself as a body of water that he could not hurt. I would offer no overt resistance so that whatever he tried to inflict on me would pass right through me, as I yielded to all pressure without a struggle.

In my third year at the gymnasium Herr Professor Wagner flunked me in Geography. This meant I had to spend my summer vacation preparing for a make-up examination in the fall. My alternative was to repeat the entire year of study, in the Austrian system, the third grade of the Gymnasium. The message finally came through to my parents, and they went to see the Herr Direktor. I took the exam in the fall, passed, and after that was free from any further contact with Wagner.

Three years of this anguish took a heavy toll. I remember my sadness, my sense of helplessness and despair. I am sure that my passive adaptation exerted a lasting impact on my personality. I am not proud that I learned to deal with irresistible authority by submitting overtly while I was secretly holding on to my self-respect. Yet, even now, I cannot think of a better way in which I could have handled the situation without allowing it to break me down.

After the war I learned that Herr Professor Wagner had fallen on the Russian front. I cannot admit to any notable grief or mourning.

Living through the "Wagner-years" might have been even harder to endure had it not been for a few good friends, my love of music, and the presence of some visiting family members from Poland, students who turned out to be sympathetic and supportive listeners. I "hung out" with three friends, with whom I played, took walks and hiked through the Vienna Woods. Occasionally, we did our homework together. We all lived in the same neighborhood and attended the same class, so they were witnesses to my ordeal and, albeit silently, cheered me on. We truly cared about each other.

One of them, George, was even closer to me than the others. He was a slender, tall boy, quiet-voiced with blond hair and blue eyes.

Through the years his appearance did not seem to change much and tended to remind people of the actor Leslie Howard. He too was an only child, very bright, and most important to me, he, too, was passionately involved with music. We played through most of the Beethoven and Schubert symphonies on his or my piano from scores for four hands and on our very long walks around the Ringstrasse, we hummed through most of the popular opera repertoire which was familiar to both of us. We attended opera performances and concerts together, standing in long queues to get good standing room places. We had a recognition code when we lost each other in a crowd. Whenever one of us whistled the opening bars of *The Rosenkavalier*, the other would know where to look. We argued passionately about our differing preferences for various composers and their creations, the "right" tempi and the "correct" phrasing; and we held heated discussions over "profound" matters of philosophy.

The German word "Weltanschauung," literally translated, means "a view of the world," but is not adequately expressed by this phrase. It means so much more and includes everything from religion to politics to the meaning or purpose of life. Somehow, with an extra dose of hubris, we felt entitled to consider these weighty issues, and made up for what we did not know by the passion of our convictions. We were not able to change the shape of things to come, but we enjoyed sharpening our debating skills.

Eventually, I was able to assist George in his escape from the Nazis. We remained friends, and continued seeing each other periodically despite his career as a musicologist and conductor which led him to live with his family on the West Coast and in the Middle West until his untimely death a few short years ago.

Opera became almost an obsession with me. I can pinpoint the event that hooked me on the lyric theater forever. I was about eight or nine when I was listening to a radio transmission of *The Valkyries* from the Vienna Opera while doing my homework. Listening then, did not, of course, mean stereo speakers broadcasting high fidelity sound; it meant wearing rudimentary earphones connected to a small detector set with a crystal that had to be poked correctly in order to bring in the station you wanted to hear. When the conductor, the celebrated Franz Schalk, approached the Magic Fire Music, something happened within me. It was an existential click of such transcending ecstasy that its echo rings in me to this day. I knew then that I wanted to re-experience this surge of excitement as long as I lived.

As I passed through adolescence and my voice descended to a bass pitch, the possibility that I might actually be able to make music my profession appeared very tempting; and I was encouraged by those who heard me. As soon as it was possible, my parents offered me the chance to take singing lessons, though there was never any doubt that a boy of my background would not be allowed to rest his future security on the vagaries of a musical career alone. As in the States, talent for the arts was admired, something to be nourished, to be proud of; but the arts were not viewed as a safe base on which an all-important livelihood could be built. For that you were expected to go into the professions like law or medicine, or possibly, into business.

Mother had an extended family in Poland. Some of the younger members, especially the children of the wealthier branch, came to Vienna to study at the university. They usually stayed with us until they found their own quarters, and after that were frequent visitors. For me, two of them filled the vacant place of an older brother. Ada was about nine years older than I, very much wiser, and a wonderful companion and guiding friend. Uri had come to Vienna to seek treatment with Sigmund Freud, whose home and office were around the corner from our apartment. Uri was a very gentle and kind man; as I learned later, he was impotent. He seemed to enjoy my company as much as I enjoyed his. We spent many hours together, while he allowed me to ventilate my often unhappy feelings about the situation at school and how I felt about it. He even attempted to respond to my existential questions about the goals and the meaning of life. I was very fond of both of these men who became the substitute brothers I never had.

When Uri was ready to return to Poland, my father and I

accompanied him to the railroad station to see him off. We learned the next day that he had committed suicide by hanging after his arrival home.

Ada returned to Poland after finishing his studies. He and the rest of his family disappeared without a trace during the holocaust.

Eventually, these years of "Weltschmerz" faded into the past. Herr Professor Wagner no longer was in a position to humiliate me and make my life miserable. My body changed, I became taller and stopped being the "fat kid." My interests increasingly focused on the mysteries of the opposite sex and how they affected me.

As adolescents in Vienna, we were just as obsessed with sex as boys and girls anywhere else. Yet, a number of factors specific to the time such as the historical context and the prevailing economics, gave us a somewhat different set of norms to guide us. The turmoil following World War I led to a change of sexual mores, such as happened in the United States following World War II. In the liberal middle class and upper middle class environment that I lived in, there was a considerable loosening of the previously harsh and rigid attitudes toward sexual relationships. The shortage of money encouraged a sort of camaraderie; our close association with the girls in coed classes led to a strong sense of equality, mutual concern and respect. I might view the young woman sitting next to me as an object of erotic fantasy, but, having shared the anxieties of exams and quizzes with her, I also appreciated her human side: her fears and her relief when the pressure stopped.

It was understood that all dating was "dutch" with expenses divided, a shared experience among equals. We had exquisite sexual daydreams involving the girls we "went with," and were erotically preoccupied with them, but we also were very much aware that they were our social peers and our educational colleagues. They were people first, and sex objects second.

When my friends and I talked about sex and females, which we did rather extensively, our thoughts centered on how best to invite love and desire from an equal and willing partner. I desperately envied those boys who were blessed with older sisters who, I thought, could and would initiate them into the mysteries of the female psyche so that they would know the right thing to say or do.

The notion of "scoring" with a date after drinking to "take advantage of her" was not only unacceptable, it was seen as reprehensible. To spend money on a date in order to induce sexual favors was considered repugnant. While our fantasies were stimulated by the many prostitutes who solicited along Vienna's main streets, we found them unattractive and neither I, nor as far as I could tell, any of my friends even considered engaging them. That was for those "too old" to be wanted for themselves.

As most of us did not own cars, we made love perilously in the most absurd places: on park benches, in the Vienna Woods, under bridges over the Danube, in opera and theater boxes, or any place where darkness would provide some privacy. Rain, cold or snow did not seem to matter. There was little comfort, a lot of anxiety, tremendous fatigue, but also huge fun and excitement.

But these experiences really came much later, following long periods of preoccupation trying to understand what all the fuss was about. I had read a lot about all the exciting things females concealed in those places where boys had their sex organs; all the sexy books made raving references to those hidden delights. My problem was that I did not have the slightest idea what they were writing about. Consciously, at least, I was totally in the dark about sexual differences, and, for reasons that are not at all clear to me, I was unwilling to ask. We had a small bronze statuette of a female nude mounted on a marble base on my father's desk. I recall vividly my careful examination of her groin area, hoping to find some clue, and puzzling about what may have been censored so that I would not find out the real secret. I must have been thinking of the ubiquitous fig leaf that tended to conceal the male genitals on so many art works. That there may not be any external organ at all was totally inconceivable and never occurred to me then. At some point, as I grew up, this mystery was clarified, and I wish I could remember how and when.

Once this basic secret was revealed, another puzzle challenged my curiosity. How did boys and girls manage to kiss without bumping their noses? I had heard that Eskimos were supposed to kiss by rubbing their noses together, or by tickling each other's cheeks with the fluttering of their eyelashes. That, I thought, would certainly make things easier. The whole idea became more and more intriguing as time went on, and soon gave way to anxiety that I might be fatally clumsy in my first attempt to risk an experiment.

Reading added to my confusion. Alternately, boys/men who tried to kiss girls/women were depicted as nasty, dirty villains whose faces got slapped; or, they were romantic heroes whom the desired lady first fought off, just as in the first scenario, but then passionately welcomed. How was a boy to know? Eventually, this, too, was somehow resolved.

My first, truly romantic crush came when I had just passed thirteen and met a lovely young lady of my own age. We took long walks in the Prater, Vienna's large park and amusement area. We talked a lot, stood in line for standing room tickets at the opera, and exchanged extravagant letters professing our affection for each other and our views of the world. After a lot of fantasizing, I even exchanged a chaste lip-to-lip kiss with Edith, and was sure that I had been transformed into an adult.

Edith's father seemed concerned about his daughter's adventures and always met us at the street car stop when I brought her home from the opera. Once, some Nazis exploded a stink bomb at the opera house which had to be emptied for an airing. The opera resumed about forty five minutes later, and, of course, we were late arriving at Edith's stop. Her father, understandably upset, gave me an icy look and said: "Mr. Hecht, I would have expected better from you." At thirteen, I even thought he might be right.

Music played a large part in our friendship which lasted about three months. The interlude of Mascagni's *Cavalleria Rusticana* will forever be associated in my heart with the great emotional throbbing I felt when I held hands with Edith. When we broke off after an exchange of letters, I consoled myself by playing and singing the saddest parts of Schumann's song cycle, the "Dichterliebe," the love of poets.

My wounds must have healed quickly, because I then fell in

love with Jenny. She was sixteen, my friend Alfred's older sister. Jenny was my ideal of adult, mature womanhood. With her charm and sophistication, she embodied all the glamor and mystique I had come to expect of females. Together we listened to American records conducted by Stokowsky and discussed such weighty concepts as religion fulfilling a human need to understand what otherwise could not be grasped. I sat at Alfred's side soaking in all this wisdom and wishing nothing more fervently than to change places with him so that I could be in Jenny's presence more often. For months, I lived to see her and to impress her. Once, she kissed me on the cheek. I was besotted enough not to wash my face for days.

Soon, the bittersweet era of romantic innocence gave way to more defined and focused sexual interest. In the summer of 1934 my parents arranged for a student exchange with Jean, a French boy of my age from Rochefort sur Mer, not far from Bordeaux. I was to spend the first five weeks of my summer vacation with him and his family, and he would then spend the rest of the summer with us in Vienna. The purpose of the trip was to enable us to refine our language skills; in fact, at the end of my trip I spoke an accent free, native sounding French. More important than the language, this was my first time away from home, my chance to be abroad, and my freedom to experience all the adventures I was ready for as I approached sixteen. The very first day and night of the trip offered the unexpected fulfillment of adolescent fantasies and changed me forever. My parents took me to the station where I boarded the international express to Paris. There were many other teens, also bound for their vacations in Switzerland or France on the same train. Not long after departure, I felt restless and walked the length of the corridors into which European train compartments open.

Before long I fell into conversation with a, to me, "glamorous" young woman of about eighteen or nineteen who clearly did not realize that I was not yet sixteen. Erica was a beautiful blond with high Slavic cheekbones and green eyes. She had just been graduated from the gymnasium and was about to enter a renowned actors' school that the director Max Reinhardt had established in Vienna. She, too, was on her first solo trip abroad, and she, too, was ready for adventure. The details of our encounter remain very vivid in my memory, perhaps because in the years ahead I so often relived that night on the train in my mind.

Our conversation soon proceeded from a discussion of books we had read and liked to more personal subjects, and before long, we kissed and embraced. Erica had been involved with the father of one of her girlfriends, and was not only older but also a lot more experienced than I. Somehow, I managed not to divulge my true age and succeeded in inviting Erica's interest. We spent the entire evening and night loving and exploring each other while the train hurled through the length of Austria and Switzerland. A sympathetic conductor accepted a small bribe and provided an empty first class compartment where we could have some privacy. I was overwhelmed by Erica's willing intimacy, her sensuality and sophistication. When she offered to revive me from total exhaustion with a swig from a flask of cognac, I felt I had entered a world of glamor that I believed existed only in my dreams. About four hours before we reached Paris, Erica left for her destination, and I knew that I had fallen in love. I also suspected that I would lose her soon after our return to Vienna, as she would inevitably discover my real age.

That's what happened. We saw each other a few times until the moment of truth could no longer be postponed. We remained good friends, and I survived my hurt and frustration and continued to draw some pleasure from my memories. Erica, in time, became a rather famous actress and risked her career to meet me for a last farewell before I left Vienna in 1938. She had a few years of international recognition after the war, married a stage director who had been connected to the Communists, and eventually disappeared from the scene after the Russian occupation of Vienna ended. Our often shared fantasy of meeting twenty years later for a passionate week on the Riviera, I as a famous singer, she as a great actress, never was realized.

My first view of the city of Paris was exhilarating. I appreciated its beauty, felt its vibrant vitality, and gloried in the excitement of roaming the boulevards before changing train stations for Rochefort. This was an enthralling introduction.

With my French host family and my contemporary, Jean, I found a hospitable home. I absorbed the French language, learned to eat mussels and crayfish, to drink wine with my water, to bicycle all over the countryside; I had my first view of the ocean and beaches, I danced in the streets on Bastille Day and met some delightful and charming French girls. It was Raymonde, herself quite virginal, who led me to a secluded spot in the middle of a wheat field, where under a hot noonday sun in July, we clumsily but lovingly satisfied our curiosity about national differences in love making. Both of us seemed quite pleased to leave things at that; in contrast to my deep preoccupation with Erica, I thought fondly, but quite unemotionally, about Raymonde, and believed that she did not feel differently about me.

During my stay in France, I learned from the radio and newspapers that there had been a Nazi uprising in Vienna on July 25, that it had been put down by the army, that the Prime Minister, Mr. Dollfuss, had been assassinated, that the Nazi party had been outlawed, and that martial law had been declared. After I was reassured by telephone that my parents and all those I cared about were unhurt, life continued pleasantly for me. What made the power of denial especially incredible was that we all knew that the government of Austria rested on the support of about five percent of the population, and on the indifference of about ten percent. Roughly forty percent belonged to, or sympathized with, the Nazis, and another forty five percent belonged to, or sympathized with, the Social Democrats who were also outlawed.

On my return to Vienna with Jean the city seemed especially lovely. It was good to be back home. One August evening, a few friends and I stood on the terrace of the Burgtheater during the intermission of a play. We were facing the Ring, the eclectic Gothic spire of the City Hall surrounded by parks. To the left was the Greek temple of the parliament building, to the right, the sprawling complex of Vienna University, all of it bathed in the golden glow of the setting sun. I was flooded with love for my city, and very proud to show it off to my French friend, Jean. This was August 1934, almost exactly four years before I was overjoyed that I had the opportunity to leave this same city alive, a refugee on his way to permanent exile.

With the beginning of the new school year, life resumed its established routine. I began to be invited to numerous parties by the young women I had met at social occasions, our ice skating group or tennis club. In the spring there were dances and balls, and soon my name began to appear as a member of the "committees" that suggested the lists of others to be invited.

I was accepted at the State Academy of Music, where I studied piano and music theory with one of Austria's foremost composers, Joseph Marx, who habitually appeared forty-five minutes late for his classes, exclaiming: "Sorry, I had to attend a meeting."

Soon I acquired a "steady" girlfriend, Alice, and we spent most of our free time together, taking walks, sitting in coffee houses, going to concerts, opera, movies, and petting and making love in the most exotic and bizarre places. "Nice" girls did not go to hotels with boys; also, hotels would have cost money we did not have. Opportunities for privacy at our family homes or the homes of our friends were very rare; as a consequence we drew heavily on our ingenuity and creativity to discover more or less suitable places where we could surreptitiously pet and make love. Standing room at the opera and Vienna's many parks and movie houses ranked high on our lists.

Shortly before I was to take the final exam at the Gymnasium, the Matura, I walked Alice home from a dance, and we stopped at a bench in the Stadtpark at about three a.m. Suddenly a policeman emerged from behind some dark bushes to find us heavily engaged with each other and in an embarrassing state of undress. Without giving us much pause, he interrogated us separately, asking each other's name and address to "ascertain that the lady is not a professional" whom I had just picked up. He finally let things rest after suggesting we get properly dressed. Not only was I mortified by the shame and embarrassment of the situation and my own helplessness, I had to be concerned about whether a police report to the school might not interfere with my impending graduation. Fortunately, this episode just became another memory from the times when we danced on top of the volcano.

Eventually, the relationship with Alice came to an end. We remained friends, and it was through her that I was able to acquire the coveted affidavit necessary to obtain an American immigration visa.

During these later teenage years, life proceeded in an almost routine fashion. The days were filled with schoolwork, partly at the gymnasium, partly at the music academy, with private French and English lessons, homework, piano practice, and private singing lessons. Whatever free time there was, and there always was some, was spent taking walks with Alice, meeting friends, going to movies, theaters, concerts and opera performances. For anyone looking in from the outside, it must have seemed the perfect mixture of education, fun and recreation, a full use of the wonderful opportunities a city like Vienna offered. And in some ways it was so.

Yet, somewhere deep down within us, there was a barely conscious anxiety, a vague perception of the unnatural state of affairs that surrounded us. Try as we did to suppress or deny the existence of the damned up rage around us, we could not escape the news accounts of growing anti-Semitic actions in Germany, now ruled by Hitler, and could not totally blind ourselves to the instability of our own situation in Austria.

I knew that, starting in 1934, I was living in a fascist state with a conservative authoritarian government that tried to follow the Italian fascist model. The Austrian government, however, did not have the charismatic figure of a Mussolini to inspire support; it had just enough of an armed force to suppress the various attempts to overthrow it. In the face of takeover threats from our powerful neighbor to the north, Nazi Germany, we consoled each other with reassurances that Italy, Czechoslovakia, and the mighty Western powers would "never allow such a thing."

The dictatorship imposed by the "Patriotic Front," the political arm of the government, required adaptations for which my experience with Professor Wagner had well prepared me. Most of the Jewish kids of my background tended to be sympathetic to the left, to the banned Social Democrats and the labor unions. Some continued to be politically active and went underground, some were arrested and spent time in jail. Others, and I am not proud to confess that I belonged to that group, figuratively closed their eyes and concentrated on the business of survival under stress.

The most elementary activities began to become conditional on pledges of loyalty to the super patriotic government. To continue matriculation at the university, one had to take a series of exams on patriotism and on a biased version of Austrian history. To qualify for membership in the most innocuous youth groups, for example, an organization to get cheaper standing room tickets for the opera and theaters, I was asked to sign pledges of loyalty to the Patriotic Front. I wrestled with myself for a few days, but eventually, I rationalized myself into surrender by questioning the utility of resisting blackmail. It was not too difficult to make fun of the regulations, to make jokes about them and mock them, even to wink at the enforcers who not infrequently winked back. Yet, deep down, I was uncomfortable and ashamed of myself for not protesting and for running away from the disagreeable consequences I was able to avoid by not standing up courageously for my convictions.

So I joined most of my friends in making the necessary compromises. With great, mostly unconscious determination, we ignored the portents of doom that were staring us in the face. A great number of our neighbors and colleagues were not so secretive about plotting our downfall; it must have taken a great deal of energy to look away, and live from day to day as if these were the happiest of times. The end of the world as we had known it was around the corner; the signs were clear. Nobody observing me and my behavior could have suspected any of that. Studies, tennis, vacations, parties, all the time-honored pleasures of youth and dreams of a glorious future easily surpassed frightening worries concerning a menacing tomorrow.

As the end of the gymnasium years approached, some decisions about my professional choices had to be made. My parents were eager and willing to support my goals. While they did not discourage my interest in music and what appeared to be a potentially professional talent for singing, they placed a strong emphasis on the need for some more tangible educational credentials.

When I was about thirteen, I had read Sinclair Lewis' *Arrowsmith*. I was impressed by the calling of the novel's hero and became more and more inspired to consider a career as a physician. Everything about Dr. Arrowsmith's character fascinated me: his research efforts, his struggles and his idealism, all combined to make me want to emulate him.

A few years later, another book, Stephan Zweig's *Heilung durch den Geist*, (Healing through the Spirit) had a strong impact on me. The book presented three short biographies of personalities who prepared the way to what Zweig saw as the scientific approach of treating the mind, psychoanalysis. He traced the development from Mesmer and his extensive use of hypnotism, via Mary Baker Eddy and her healing through Christian Science, to Freud and his efforts to present an encompassing theory of personality, from which then could flow a clinical method of healing.

I was intrigued by the ideas the book presented, and went on to read Freud's *Interpretation of Dreams*, fascinated by what I learned. Psychoanalysis was a much discussed subject among my contemporaries in Vienna. We didn't really understand much about it; yet, the concepts, the language, and, perhaps the frankness with which Freud approached human sexuality impressed me powerfully. The Freud family were our neighbors, and there was some gossipy interest in the Herr Professor who had his hair cut by the same barber who cut mine.

One of my dreams was to study medicine, to specialize in psychiatry, and eventually to become a psychoanalyst. The other dream, of course, was to become an opera singer. I resolved to prepare for both as much as this was possible. One of my life's ironies was that, after a number of detours and unexpected twists and turns, many years later a large part of both those dreams came true.

I took to medical school as a fish would take to water. I loved everything about it. The atmosphere of dedicated professional preparation, the challenges of colloquia on short notice, the constant supervision in the laboratories and the dissecting halls, the learning about the anatomy and physiology of the human body, the camaraderie among the colleagues, all filled me with excitement and wonder. Being treated as an adult, wearing the white coat that identified me as a prospective member of an honored profession, the opportunity to audit classes that included attendance at complicated surgical procedures, obstetrics, dermatology and psychiatry all proved exhilarating and highly stimulating.

In the first two years our required curriculum was preclinical, but our enthusiasm was such that we went to the clinical demonstrations in our free time. I also volunteered to spend time dissecting during the official vacations, and enjoyed every moment of it.

At the advanced age of nineteen, I had an almost obsessive infatuation with Daisy, my colleague and dissecting partner at Medical School. Though not remarkably pretty, Daisy possessed an immense natural magnetism. Highly intelligent, she actively cultivated many interests, including ballet, music and literature. Her very affluent family made it possible for her to pursue any endeavor she wished, and she seemed to excel in everything. Romantically, she was unapproachable beyond pleasant cama-raderie. All the boys I knew had a crush on her. In spite of all their efforts, none, to my knowledge, were more successful in getting Daisy to respond than I. While we were separated during summer vacations, I wrote her love letters, confessing my longing for her. She answered in a friendly, somewhat removed noncommittal manner.

For more than a year, Daisy was foremost in my mind and heart while I experienced all the tortures of romantic unrequited love. Some forty years later, Daisy visited the United States from

Australia where she had survived the holocaust. We were both invited for dinner at the house of a mutual friend. In shock I beheld my beloved Daisy, a rather drab, motherly, mildly depressed widow who seemed to have stopped growing a long time before. Somewhat coquettishly, she produced from her handbag a few of the letters I had written to her back then. Belatedly, I knew I had made more of an impression on her than I suspected.

My positive feelings about medical school were enhanced by a tradition that made all professors (some were of world renown) address the medical students as "colleague." Another, typically Viennese style, dictated that all waiters would address students as "doctor," a custom that did not noticeably diminish the sense of self-importance among the eighteen and nineteen-year-olds. Once you got your doctorate, it was understood that those same waiters in the coffee houses around the university would address you as "Herr Professor."

And so it went, past the comprehensive exams at the end of the second semester which I passed with distinction, right into the beginning of the fourth semester.

The oral exams were held in public, and could cover any aspect of the subject. They were usually attended by students who were waiting to take them and hoped to get some clues from the questions the professor posed. The Professor who examined me in Physics was a Nobel prize nominee and not particularly stimulated by examining his young students. He had a reputation for formulating his first question, around which he then built the rest of the exam, by taking clues from the name of the student or from the occupation of the student's father. My name, Hecht, meant pike in German. I was superbly prepared to hold forth on the physics of how fishes swam. As soon as I sat down, Professor Ehrenhaft looked at my record, said: "Hm, your name is Hecht, hmm, Dr. Hecht, talk to me about how fishes swim." I did. And what a time we had celebrating our successful completion of the first two semesters! A group of us went up into the Vienna woods to an elegant restaurant on the Kobenzl; we ate and drank and were merry until the wee hours of the morning. And then we danced down the mountain, arm in arm, Daisy and I, into Grinzing, and ended up in the city having breakfast in one of the cellar cafés.

On the eve of Hitler's takeover in February 1938, I attended the famous Vienna Opera Ball, the highlight of the Carnival season, wearing borrowed tails and white tie and dancing through the night. "Those were the days, my friend, we thought they'd never end..."

III — "I LIFT MY LAMP..."

Patriotism, love of country, allegiance to the flag are lofty, high sounding concepts. I have often thought of them as meaningless, much abused, falsely pious phrases, and empty rituals. Yet, my feelings that morning on August 17, 1938, as the S.S. Rex steamed into New York Harbor, could be described in those terms. I felt sentimental about the Star Spangled Banner, and a deep commitment to the land that was offering me refuge and hospitality.

The high towers of lower Manhattan became visible through the morning mist as the Statue of Liberty emerged on the port side. As I stood on the deck, all the upheaval and turmoil of the last months gave way to a powerful gush of hope, and promises of freedom, equality, opportunity. All I had ever read or heard about America: its history, its people, the idealistic policies under F.D.R., flooded through me at this unforgettable hour.

People who do not approach these shores as fugitives from undeserved persecution cannot fully appreciate how powerfully proud of this country I felt, and how deeply loyal and committed to it I became. None of the realities I encountered later, whether they were racism, prejudice, bigotry or corruption, ever shook my firm belief that, imperfect as it may be, this is the best way of life to be found in today's world.

On board ship I had my first encounter with spontaneous American generosity. One of the passengers, a very dignified, distinguished looking, middle-aged gentleman of Irish ancestry, a judge from Cleveland, was returning from a European vacation. He seemed interested in my background. In one conversation, I mentioned some of my close friends who were hoping to get the magic "affidavit" so that they might apply for a quota number which, in turn, would open the way to an American visa. He interrupted my account with a few questions about their age, and how they would expect to support themselves. He offered to sponsor two of them: did, in fact, do so, and saved their lives. Unfortunately, immigration laws precluded help for my parents.

I had no plans for the immediate future, beyond getting off the ship and finding a place to bed down, but I was clear about three principal goals.

I needed to survive. That meant, I had to find a place to live and to deposit my belongings. I had to find a way to feed myself, earn some money, and, of course, find some sort of job; any job.

Second, and urgently, I needed to arrange, in whatever way I could, to bring my parents over. Time was running out for them, and I knew that it would not be easy to find sponsors who would sign affidavits for older people. A younger person could more reasonably be expected to pull his own weight. Because my parents were born in pre-World War I Polish territory, they came under the Polish immigration quota, which, in contrast to the Austrian quota, was very small and filled. I was prepared to encounter serious difficulties even after obtaining affidavits and could only hope that some political pressure might result in emergency measures that would recognize the extraordinary situation in Austria.

Third, and further ahead, I hoped to lay some groundwork that would eventually enable me to rise above the menial existence of an immigrant refugee. Remote as it seemed then, I clung to a thread of hope that there might be a chance for further education, perhaps even continuation of medical school, or some opportunities for a musical career.

In Vienna I had met a number of Russian refugees in flight from the Bolshevik revolution. Most of them were charming, intelligent, sophisticated people whose heart and soul were Russian. They represented members of an alien "emigre" group who, clinging to each other, would forever remain foreigners in any country but Russia, always longing to return to their homeland.

I was determined not to let this happen to me. I wanted to be an American, I wanted to "belong" and to shed anything that connected me to Austrian roots and the German language.

I decided I would not speak German if I could help it and would try to find American friends. In fact, when I eventually met some of my Viennese friends and colleagues, we tended to flock together, but then as now we spoke only English to each other. I am sure that, on a deeper level, we felt betrayed by the people and the culture we thought we had been part of. The language we grew up in, the accent we were stuck with for life, represented not a mother tongue, but stood for the enemy, the killers and tormentors who persecuted us.

Not until much later did I understand that my aspirations to blend into the American scene, to feel that I really belonged, were somewhat overambitious. Much as I tried, I succeeded only partially in achieving a sense of full identity.

At nineteen and a half, I was too old to have shared the important early life and school experiences of the young people in my new environment, and too young to have established firm and lasting roots in my native country. I soon thought in the English language, dressed and behaved as the people around me did, and made some efforts not to be outwardly distinguishable. But eventually, I came to acknowledge that it was too late in my life to make a full transition. Those first nineteen years made a difference, whether I liked it or not.

I knew that I could never again fit comfortably into the Austrian scene; but, I also knew in my heart of hearts that I would forever feel somewhat alien in the American environment. The refugees who arrived here at thirty or more often continued to live in an essentially transplanted European mode. I was not comfortable with that. Even at the risk of ending up "neither fish nor fowl," I had no doubt that I wished to Americanize myself as much as possible. Here I was then, at the pier in New York with a few extra dollars that I had been permitted to draw from the remnants of my shipboard account. My papers had been in order, the kind couple who had sponsored me had come to meet me, had pressed a ten dollar bill into my hand, and had wished me good luck in the new world. I was admitted quickly as a legal immigrant and now was on my own.

I had learned in Vienna that two New York organizations could be counted on to provide some aid to new immigrants. One was the Hebrew Immigrant Aid Society (HIAS); the other was the National Refugee Service (NRS). HIAS was reputed to provide shelter and food; NRS arranged for job counseling and emergency loans.

As my most immediate need was for shelter, I proceeded to the HIAS, then located in downtown New York, at the present site of the Public Theater. Looking out from the taxi that drove me and my steamer trunks to Lafayette Street, I caught sight of what was probably the ugliest part of New York, the west side stretch along the piers with its old and dilapidated houses. My spirits sank.

At the HIAS I was given a friendly reception, offered a clean bed, and was served a very palatable dinner. My spirits lifted; yet, I recognized that there was a problem I had to deal with urgently. Most of the men surrounding me (I remember no women there) were quite old, and obviously had failed to establish a life for themselves. Most of them had come from Eastern Europe in the immigration waves before World War I, and were relying on the shelter to keep them alive. They were warm and friendly to me, and God knows I needed that, but they also exuded an oppressive aura of hopelessness and broken spirit. I knew immediately that to muster the initiative and drive necessary to meet my new challenges, I had to leave this environment quickly.

However, I shall be forever grateful to the HIAS for allowing me to know that, were I to be down and out, I could count on them to provide food and lodging. I never needed to do that, but the knowledge that I could have returned provided a safety net that sustained me.

The next morning I went to the National Refugee Service, then on 46th Street and Broadway, in the middle of New York's Times Square. I thought I could walk there; after all, I was already on Broadway, and the address I was going to was on Broadway. I soon discovered that in New York, two places on the same Broadway were not necessarily within walking distance.

As I emerged from the subway on Times Square, I was overwhelmed by a multitude of impressions. Here, in full daylight reality, was the place of my dreams. How often had I seen it in the

American movies we had loved in Vienna, how often had I read about it?! I almost expected Fred Astaire, Ginger Rogers or Eleanor Powell to come dancing around the corner. As I was swept up by the crowd on the sidewalk, I felt the powerful sense of vitality and energy emanating from all these people, moving swiftly and purposefully.

As I entered the building on 46th Street, I was faced with another new phenomenon. In Vienna, when I wished to take an elevator, I either had to summon the porter and pay him, or, in more modern settings, deposit a few required coins in a slot to gain access to the "self service" lift. Tenants of a building had keys to admit them; visitors arranged to be escorted by their host. Here, facing me were large, manned elevators that cost nothing. A crowd of newcomers, as startled as I, but without the benefit of English, stood in the lobby, pointing upwards while shouting "down," or downwards while crying "up."

At the National Refugee Service I learned a word that had no real equivalent in German. That word is "appointment" or, two words, "emergency appointment." Once you answered to: "Do you have an...?" with "yes," doors miraculously opened and there was a person waiting to talk to you!

At NRS I was given an emergency loan of $25, obtained an appointment for a job placement interview, and was on my way between shouts of "up" and "down." This money allowed me to search for a place to live.

I was advised to seek lodgings in Manhattan's Washington Heights, then a clean, well preserved neighborhood of small apartment houses around Columbia's Presbyterian Hospital. For a few years, the area had attracted refugees who had fled Germany in the early days after Hitler's takeover, and in sarcastic deference to his Third Reich, it had been dubbed "The Fourth Reich." Through ads I found a pleasant furnished room with a German Jewish immigrant family. The rent was minimal, the people pleasant and understanding. The "super" had an old car and volunteered to help me pick up my trunks at the HIAS, which made it possible for me to settle in my own space on my second day in America. As much as I would have preferred to avoid the sort of immigrant enclave the neighborhood represented to speed up my "Americanization" process, I was delighted to have found a decent room on 164th Street which served me well for my first months in the city.

Finding a job was not quite as easy, even though I was determined to take any job I could get. These were depression times. Employment agencies along Sixth Avenue, (now Avenue of the Americas) all displayed signs of "dishwasher wanted, experience necessary," and were quite serious about the experience part. A downtown department store employed only selected college graduates to run the elevators, and paid them $8 a week.

My employment interview at NRS illuminated my dilemma. Neither my background as a musician/singer, nor my interrupted medical studies, qualified me professionally. My knowledge of languages and clerical skills (I had picked up some typing and an adaptation of German shorthand into English) were apparently not at all in demand. Yet, I had too much education to demonstrate an overriding need for further funded schooling. Eventually, I was sent out for a job as "powder puff stamper" in a small workshop next door to the HIAS. There, I was instructed to stamp out round pieces of material (to be used for powder puffs) by using a die and a mallet on seven or eight layers of cloth. Five and a half days a week, eight to five thirty, for $12 a week. I was delighted. Unfortunately, I injured my hand on the second day, and that was the end of my first job.

The money I had borrowed would stretch for a short while; twenty five dollars in 1938 was probably more like $400 at the present time, but I had no time to waste before all my resources would be gone. It was time to utilize my reserve of seventy or so letters of introduction and recommendation. I had no idea how my calls would be received, and I wavered between fears of rude rejection and hopes for grand job offers. I had to plunge right in. The weather was hot and humid that August, and anybody who could get to more comfortable places was gone. I nervously approached a phone booth with a supply of nickels (then the cost of a local call).

Soon a pattern of responses evolved. Many people were not in town; nobody was rude or rejecting; most calls led to an invitation for dinner. I would not starve to death in the coming weeks as long as I could dig up the fare to get to the homes of my hosts. I encountered a great deal of graciousness, warmth, hospitality and good will. I also ate a lot, most of it very tasty, and learned about prevailing rituals. For example, it did not take me long to discover that "you must come again soon" did not necessarily imply another dinner invitation in the near future, and that "how are you?" did not require a lengthy answer.

I also received a good deal of advice, some of which proved very valuable. The matter of job offers was somewhat more complicated, especially given the precarious state of the economy. Everybody showed genuine good intentions, mostly by giving advice or referring me to others who, they hoped, might be more directly helpful.

I was eager to find out whether I could make some practical use of the Bulgarian King's letter, and, as I could barely afford the cost of a phone call to the Embassy in Washington, I contacted the Consulate in New York. The consul received me readily. After he read His Majesty's letter, he almost bowed to the floor and put himself fully at my disposal. I asked for his help in finding a job; when he inquired about the kind of position that might interest me, I remembered that the letter referred to my father as a banker, and I told him that banking would offer intriguing prospects. After a few phone calls, he arranged for an appointment with the head of Speyer and Company, a large Wall Street investment firm.

That same afternoon, dressed in my best clothes, I was ushered into the imposing large office of Mr. Speyer, in the Speyer Building. I tried to conceal my nervousness as Mr. Speyer offered me a large cigar, inquired about my crossing, volunteered that he himself was leaving for Europe the next morning, and generally tried to put me at ease. After a few minutes, he decided to come to the point, leaned towards me and asked: "How much were you thinking of investing?"

In fairness, he did not bat an eyelash when I told him that rather than consider any investments at this time I would invite his help to find an urgently needed job. He explained almost apologetically that he could not offer me anything, as the bank was about to let a number of people go, but promised to keep me in mind. True to his word, before leaving for Europe he sent me a special delivery note with some suggestions.

There were other circumstances where I experienced enormous graciousness and a sincere desire to help, even though the results were disappointing. Eventually, and only through the direct intervention of Felix Warburg, another prominent banker who had made time to see me, I landed a job as stock clerk at Bloomingdale's Department Store. For the next few months I was able to earn twelve dollars a week, enough to survive on, until the day before Christmas 1938, when I and hundreds of other "holiday extras" were fired.

Only in retrospect do I understand the extent of emotional and intellectual overload I was carrying during those first months. In addition to working to keep myself alive, I was following all possible leads to resume musical training, searching for connections that might help to get my parents out of Austria and exploring any possible directions that could advance my situation. Each day, I was learning new and exciting things about life in New York and tried to integrate my past experiences with the prevailing, often very different, norms and value systems of my new homeland. There was such an overwhelming number of new impressions to absorb that there was barely time or energy to acknowledge my pervasive anxiety.

My treasure chest of letters unlocked other doors. A letter from my father's friend, Emil Varnay, the Vienna correspondent of the New York Times, introduced me to the family of the publishers who extended a gracious welcome to me. In addition to inviting me to splendid dinners, they designated George Oakes, a young member of the family, then in charge of the advertising department, to extend hospitality to me. For a time, George, a charming, handsome, intelligent and gracious man acted like the older brother I never had. I would rush home from my job, shower, change, and join him as his guest in the family's box at the Metropolitan Opera. It was unreal. I, a penniless refugee, found myself all dressed up, in Box 28 of the famed golden horseshoe. After enjoying the performance, I was given a tour of the New York Times plant around the corner.

Eventually, though tragically too late, the Ochs family volunteered to sign affidavits to help my parents get immigration visas. A short time later, the State Department, then in charge of immigration, designated new rules that required the signers of affidavits to reveal all their sources of income in great detail. I could understand that a family of such wealth and prominence would balk at that.

George tried to think of ways through which I could advance myself; he even had a specialist on the paper put together an ad that mentioned my knowledge of languages, educational background and clerical skills, and listed a box number for replies. It was a sign of the times that only two answers were received. One offered opportunities to join a new venture requiring a small capital investment, the other sought an unpaid partner. Apparently, George could not offer me a job.

Much later, I remember attending his wedding. He went on to live and work in Europe. After many years I learned to my great sorrow that he and his wife had been tragically killed in an automobile accident.

Other letters introduced me to what was then the top echelon of New York society, widening the gap between my menial, poverty-stricken existence and the surrounding world of glamor. Again, I was received, invited and introduced all around with graciousness and hospitality. My background, because of historical events of the time, lent me an exotic quality that outweighed the barriers that, under other circumstances, would have closed those doors. I had reasonably acceptable European clothes and manners, apparently enough to admit me. Again and again, I was invited by the Van Ettens, Mrs. James Deering Fessenden and others to their Park

Avenue homes. Daisy and Winifred Rogers, elderly sisters, took a kind interest in me. They lived in a magnificent apartment on Sutton Place, overlooking the East River. Every Sunday afternoon I was invited to an open-house tea over which they presided. It was a wonderful occasion for leisurely conversation with pleasant people, all much older than I, and for the munching of open cucumber sandwiches that were delicious if not very nourishing. Daisy Rogers, who had been secretary to Ann Morgan of *the* Morgans, eventually helped me to obtain a job as clerk-secretary with the New York Lighthouse for the Blind after the Christmas firing at Bloomingdale's had left me stranded. At fifteen dollars a week, in a white collar job, I felt well on my way.

The young people I met at the "society parties" were charming, friendly and forthcoming. I suspect my foreign upbringing made it difficult to identify my background in terms familiar to them among their American peers. While I did nothing to conceal my roots, I was faced with some problems. I genuinely liked these contemporaries and they seemed very willing to accept me; yet, I felt profoundly different from them, somewhat like a fish out of water. Also, I was not just fashionably poor; I was truly penniless and just barely subsisting. Not only was there no way in which I could repay their hospitality, I could not even afford to come along on, never mind invite, a date for an evening out. I had no hesitation about accepting invitations from adults who knew my status and did not expect me to reciprocate, but people my age presented a dilemma. I learned an enormous amount about American life, values and styles while moving in social spheres that were not known for their eagerness to welcome new immigrants.

Music remained my great hope. My box of letters provided a start. Some of mother's musical colleagues had well connected friends in New York and they had given me introductory letters to them. In most instances I encountered heartwarming good will and welcome.

A letter from Carl Alvin, a conductor at the Vienna Opera and the husband of the famous Elisabeth Schumann, introduced me to

Felix Wolfes, then an assistant conductor at the Metropolitan Opera. Felix, a German Jew who had arrived in America a few years earlier, invited me to sing for him at his Riverside Drive apartment. After the first twenty minutes or so, he began to busy himself making phone calls to arrange auditions with some of the most prominent vocal teachers in New York.

We went through more music together. Before I left, he turned to me and told me that he, too, had come to the States a short time ago and knew what it was like to be broke. Would I accept his offer to lend me some money? Deeply moved, I was able to express my grateful appreciation and to decline. His spontaneous offer boosted my morale tremendously, and projected a model of kindness and generosity that I could only hope to emulate in years to come.

Felix remained a friend and advisor for a long time. In 1949, I had the privilege and satisfaction of singing The Count in Mozart's *Marriage of Figaro* in Tanglewood under his baton. Eventually, as our lives took different directions, we lost close contact.

Among the various vocal teachers for whom I was auditioning was a man of international reputation whose voice I had been admiring ever since, as a child, I discovered Wagner and began dreaming of singing the dramatic roles of the "Heldenbariton" repertoire. The legendary Friedrich Schorr was then the star of the German Department at the Metropolitan Opera. His performances as Wotan, Hans Sachs and in other Wagnerian roles had made him, beyond dispute, the world's leading performer of his genre. He had recorded most of the important Wagnerian monologues on 78s, and his records are considered valuable collectors' items even today. Because he was a Jew, and the son of a cantor, he left Germany and made his home in New York, where, with his friend, the conductor Bodanzky, he ran the German Section of the Met. When I met him, rumors were rampant that the strain of singing his most demanding roles had begun to show in his voice, especially in his higher range. In fact, there was some gossip among the small international coterie of opera fans about his "faking" important high notes by rolling the r's preceding the vowel on a prominent high note in the *Valkyries* to disguise his not singing the high F the score demanded.

Schorr was at a point in his career when he was on the verge of cutting down on performances and was thinking of a shift towards teaching. The notion of shaping young talent and imparting the benefit of his tremendous experience to young singers must have tempted him to try his hand with a select small number of students.

One day, after finishing my day's work at Bloomingdale's and changing clothes, I presented myself in the studio of my idol. Awestruck and tremulous, I ascended to the 28th floor of the Majestic Apartments on 72nd Street and Central Park West. As I left the elevator, wafts of wonderful smelling food greeted me, and I was admitted to a luxuriously furnished studio with a breath-taking view of the park. The thought that this much adored star might consider teaching me without charge quickly helped me regain my breath, and I proceeded to sing for him. Schorr did, in fact, accept me as his vocal student, and laid down a set of rules to follow. They concerned an absolute prohibition against singing anything but the exercises he gave me, and some reasonable admonitions to maintain a healthy life style. We discussed a more formal arrangement for compensation after my career would begin to take off.

My joy and exhilaration were boundless. The mere fact that my artistic idol had enough confidence in me to hold out the chance of a "career" was pretty heady stuff. Added to this, the opportunity to learn from him, and, if and when I might be found ready, to be guided by somebody with his wisdom and contacts exceeded my wildest dreams.

My letters home were jubilant; my existence began to center around my singing lessons and my biweekly pilgrimage to the wonderful food smells on Central Park West. I even began to develop the typical singer's obsessive preoccupation with his "precious" voice. My anxiety peaked when in my previous job I had to spend time out in the cold winter air without a coat, while loading merchandise unto trucks at Bloomingdale's.

Schorr was very patient and a bit stern, especially in his

insistence that I restrict myself to certain basic exercises which consisted of slow, rather rigid renditions of scales. After a while, I began to notice that my throat hurt when I was singing and that it became arduous to produce notes that began to sound labored and constricted. When I tried to bring this to my teacher's attention, he seemed displeased and I felt that I must be doing something wrong.

I shared my experience with Felix Wolfes, and through him and his contacts I was sent to see another extraordinary person, Doctor Meyer-Hermann. A large, ebullient man with a magnificent sense of humor and a very big heart, he had become famous in Berlin as *the* singers' doctor. He ministered to the world's most famous vocal cords, and his reputation and charisma were such that some artists, when suffering from vocal difficulties, would not go on stage unless they knew that he was in the wings and could be relied on to perform his magic. One of his patients had a portrait of him commissioned that is now on display at the Museum of Modern Art in New York. The waiting room of his offices on 72nd Street and Park Avenue was crowded with the famous, the not so famous, and young nobodies like myself. Dr. Meyer-Hermann refused to accept any professional fee from me, insisted on many return visits, was always ready to help and advise, and never stinted with his time or attention.

After observing my throat over a period of time, he found that I was on the verge of developing nodules on my vocal cords. Apparently, the way I was using my voice strained these tiny muscles that were vitally involved in producing sounds. Nodules were considered a serious threat to the voice. All my hopes for a career as a singer seemed suddenly in danger of being smashed before I even had the opportunity to try.

Meyer-Hermann broke the news to me as gently as possible. In his opinion, my vocal problems were due to the faulty technique of voice production I was being taught. There were no alternatives but to change teachers or to lose my voice.

I assessed my situation. I was a nineteen-year old penniless refugee without a support system, holding a temporary menial job that permitted me a tenuous survival. My hopes for betterment rested squarely on the potential use of whatever vocal talents I possessed. I needed training, guidance, and any sponsorship I could get. Unable to pay for my lessons, I had to depend on the faith and good will of any teacher willing to work with me.

Through a stroke of luck I had gained the interest of Friedrich Schorr, an influential and renowned artist who charitably had accepted me as his pupil. Yet, unless I could muster the nerve to confront him and risk his anger and disappointment, my aspirations appeared to be doomed. Beside feeling frightened, I also felt ungrateful, unappreciative of his generosity, and concerned that I might hurt or offend him. I might also invite his lasting animosity which could seriously hamper any possible chances I could have as an operatic singer.

Yet, I saw no way out. This time, with a sinking feeling of dread in my stomach, with flaming cheeks and deep embarrassment, with anxiety feelings quite different from those of only a few months ago, I approached the 28th floor of the Majestic Apartments. I blurted out that I had to say something, and could only hope that Mr. Schorr would not think of me as ungrateful. I confronted the great Schorr with what I had been told, and added that I could no longer remain his student. He hardly showed any emotion and dismissed me with some coolness and a very slight hint of bitterness. I never saw him again anywhere but on stage. He retired not very long afterwards.

Soon, with the help of interested musician friends, I obtained a scholarship with a very solid teacher, Emmy Joseph, who guided my voice for the next few years. While she did not have the prominence and glamor of Schorr, my pains in the throat stopped and there was no more talk of nodules on the vocal cords.

Soon, I had the opportunity to earn a little money by singing. Through the National Refugee Service I was sent to audition for a job as soloist with a quartet that was to sing the Jewish High Holiday Services at a Reform Temple in Long Island. I was hired, and had a wonderful time singing, apparently to the satisfaction of the congregation. I took my first train ride in America and experienced, for the first time in my life, the thrill of singing and being paid for it, and I enjoyed it all enormously.

Perhaps more importantly, the Temple's young Rabbi became my friend. He introduced me to his family and to many other young people in the community. Rabbi Harold Saperstein, who later was to become one of the outstanding Jewish leaders in the United States, helped me to arrange for affidavits for a number of my Viennese friends through members of his congregation. I became a frequent guest in his house and in the homes of his congregants, spent weekends there, was invited to bring some refugee friends along, and had the opportunity to learn about Jewish middle class life in suburbia.

Indirectly, the experience there prepared me for another important professional venture ten years later, when I became the cantor of the largest and oldest reform congregation in New Jersey. While there, I was able to pursue my career in concert and opera, and eventually, to attend graduate school and to earn my doctorate in clinical psychology at Columbia University.

My first experience as a cantor, followed by the more extensive one ten years later, caused me to reflect on my Jewish identity and my attitude toward religious ritual. I have always fully accepted my Jewish identity and heritage. This is where I came from, this has determined much of the course of my life, this is who I am, and I expect, until I die, this is what I shall remain. Issues of religious observances, nationalism, investment in traditions, while surely related, seem very separate to me.

My parents, only one or two generations removed from the ghettos of Poland, felt strongly identified as Jews, but lived their lives quite integrated into their Viennese environment. The language spoken at home was German, with only occasional lapses into Polish when they did not wish me to understand what they were saying. Of course, before long I picked up enough Polish to comprehend what I was not supposed to. With the exception of special rituals related to mourning over the loss of family, their religious observances consisted of fasting on Yom Kippur, the Day of Atonement, and of eating splendid, festive meals at the time of the Jewish New Year. I do not believe that either of them knew Hebrew, or had more than a smattering of Yiddish, a language which through many of its pithy expressions had entered colloquial Viennese German.

Religious instructions were obligatory in the Austrian school system, which meant that for two hours a week our classes were divided by religious denominations (Catholic, Protestant, Jewish), instructed by an outside teacher. Neither I nor my friends became deeply involved in religious study, but some rudimentary acquaintance with Hebrew, Jewish tradition and history was absorbed, and contributed to my sense of identity.

The Jewish Community of Vienna distributed a book to all elementary school pupils which made a lasting impression on me. It was *Graetz's History of the Jews*. His vivid accounts of the past persecutions and expulsions of Jews all over the world, as well as his accounts of heroic acts, steadfast martyrdom and inspired leadership filled me with great emotion and resolve to emulate these idealistic ancestors. My fantasies were frighteningly stimulated by accounts of the Auto da Fe's and tortures of the Spanish Inquisition. Some of these terrors were reinforced when, as a child I saw on stage the burning of Jews at the stake in Halevy's opera *La Juive*, with my mother in a leading role. A somewhat similar reaction, somehow associated with the scent of stage smoke, occurred when I witnessed the burning of the heretics in Verdi's *Don Carlo*. Perhaps this is one of the not very rational reasons why I do not wish to be cremated after my demise. Of course, in those days I could not have the slightest inkling how closely history was to repeat itself in my lifetime; in fact, in the not very distant future.

I always felt a bond of unity with my fellow Jews based, I believe, on various elements. There was our long common past as victims of oppression and persecution, there was pride of our having survived through the ages in spite of all vicissitudes, and there was also pride in our history of intellectual and scientific achievements. These considerations outweighed the many differences among the various groups of Jews.

When my father's mother died, he decided to attend the prescribed daily services and, in the morning and evening went to the synagogue to recite the prayer for the dead, the "Kaddish." I enjoyed accompanying him very much; I felt the approving looks of the other worshipers, sensed my father's pleasure in my company, and liked feeling as if I were an adult among other adults. Although the rapid recitation of prayers that I could neither follow nor understand tried my attention span, I often felt moved by the music chanted by cantor and choir.

Between the ages of eight and thirteen, I went through a period of strong religious interest, fasted on the day of atonement to the delight of my parents, and attended youth services at the temple. With the arrival of adolescence, my friends and I became quite involved in discussions about religion, its origin, its use and so on. Soon I began to recognize how religion could represent a construct that accommodated a variety of powerful human needs; especially the needs to find explanations for the inexplicable mysteries of life, birth and death; the need to find support when faced with fears of an unpredictable future, and the wish for ongoing parental protection which would be granted in return for acceptable behavior.

In our youthful arrogance we determined that religious teachings might be useful crutches for those who had to cling to them and could believe in them. *We*, with the feelings of omnipotence and immortality so characteristic of adolescents, felt above such things. My faith as well as my attendance at youth services diminished rapidly.

At thirteen, when I was confirmed and officially became a Bar Mitzvah, a "Son of the Commandments," I cared a lot more about the social functions and presents that accompanied the ceremonies than about their spiritual and religious meaning.

It seemed to me there were more divisions among Jews here than there had been in Austria, often relevant to their country of origin. I found myself more on the edge than in the mainstream of any group, unable to quite "fit" into a specific pattern. The Eastern European Jews, mostly from Russia and Poland, spoke Yiddish primarily and were more observant of religious practices than the Jews I had known in Vienna. They had fled from persecution which generated more political awareness among their youths who were often strongly to the left of the political spectrum. Many in this group harbored deep resentments against the German Jews who had preceded them and had been able to establish a secure foothold in this country. Some of the "Germans" had become successful, assimilated and were somewhat embarrassed by their cultural and social differences with the newer immigrants. Because my accent was German, I was often thought of as a member of that group.

All these factions and those who belonged to various shades of beliefs inbetween, received me with great warmth and hospitality. The "German Jews" also welcomed me most graciously, and while my own upbringing helped me to relate easily to them, I felt that I had as much or as little in common with them as I had with the descendants of the Polish and Russian Jews. I certainly had no claim to social or financial status of any kind and it was easy to belong to the edges of all the various groups. But, I also knew that, in truth, I belonged to none of them. In spite of all we had in common, I felt different and could not readily fit my background to theirs.

Emotionally, I react to religion in more complex ways. Throughout my life I have responded much more strongly to the "music than to the words." In musical terms, messages of awe, suffering, pleading, hope, sadness or transcendence strike strongly reactive strings. Sincerely felt, "good" religious music, be it the chanting of the cantor, the Passions by Bach, the Requiems by Berlioz, Brahms, Mozart, Verdi, or Faure, the Missa Solemnis by Beethoven, the Service by Bloch, all can excite the core of my emotional being. As long as I am not challenged to deal critically with the words, I can fully relate with sincerity and nostalgia to the feelings of the religious music I am singing.

The first few months in New York were filled from moment to moment with wondrous discoveries. It seemed that everything any heart desired was easily available. Whether you longed for beaches, climbs along the Hudson, superb museums, parks, endless varieties of exotic foods, architectural marvels, or any kind of entertainment, all was available at amazingly minimal cost. During those days of great economic depression, New York, then more tranquil than now, could offer you the world, often for no more than a nickel for subway, bus or ferry.

For someone like me who always had been blessed (or plagued) with great interest in edibles, the local food delights were quite new and startling. For ten cents I could purchase three delicious pancakes with butter and syrup, could watch them being flipped and then fill my stomach for quite a few hours. Nothing had prepared me for the likes of thick milkshakes or ice cream sodas. I soon discovered that fifteen cents could buy a more than adequate breakfast of orange juice, a cream cheese sandwich on datenut bread and coffee at "Chock Full o'Nuts." A sandwich purchase in a cafeteria allowed me not only to linger in a well heated place, but provided unlimited access to shelves of free cole slaw and condiments. A ten-cent glass of beer at any of the numerous White Rose Bars included a "free lunch." In contrast to Vienna, where every piece of bread or butter was carefully noted on the check, restaurants offered all the free bread and butter I could want.

I fondly recall a three-course lunch, including egg roll and lobster which I consumed at a Chinese restaurant on Lexington Avenue near Bloomingdale's, that cost 25 cents. A full five-course meal at a rather nice French place on Lexington Avenue and 54th Street, the "Boulevard de Paris," cost 50 cents. I could eat most adequately for a dollar a day.

Then, there were the sights of New York. In contrast to my first shock at seeing the dilapidated buildings along my drive from the pier to the HIAS, I now beheld Rockefeller Center. This huge complex seemed like one of the wonders of the world; in my mind, I compared the concept of its buildings and plazas to the Piazza San Marco in Venice. When I took a walk around my neighborhood in Washington Heights, I would come to Riverside Park in the 160s. Any evening, I could look South along the lit-up west side of Manhattan; I could watch the moving ribbons of light on the Westside Highway to my left, the reflections on the broad waters of the Hudson River in front of me and the glittering sparkle of the George Washington Bridge on my right. The brilliance and sense of vitality were awesome.

And there was Central Park, with lawns you were permitted to walk on; Fifth Avenue with all the majestic buildings, and the double-decker buses that, for a nickel, you could ride in the open summer air, all the way from Washington Square to the Cloisters. The exciting view of the midtown skyline that could be seen from the 86th Street Central Park Transverse; and, of course, there were the magnificent museums, none of which, as I recall it, then charged admission.

I reserved a special place in my heart for the Frick Collection, a former privately owned mansion, now open to the public, which housed air-conditioned indoor gardens, pools, concerts, and an incredible collection of some of the world's finest paintings. I spent many serene moments in this marvelous place; a quiet refuge from the hustle and bustle outside. I loved it all. What can equal the impact of the first visit to Radio City Music Hall! The mind boggled at the richness and abundance of presentations. A full Corps de Ballet, a symphony orchestra, huge production numbers, Vaudeville stars, opera singers such as Jan Peerce, the un-believable precision of those magnificent looking women, the Rockettes, and to boot, a first run movie on the giant screen. All this in comfortable seats and in an almost luxurious atmosphere, for about a dollar and twenty five cents!

The local populace took it all for granted. Seen through my eyes at that time, it all bordered on the miraculous. Many years later, in the early fifties, I appeared on the stage of the Radio City Music Hall to sing the Toreador in excerpts from *Carmen,* four times a day for two weeks. By then, experiencing it all through the back stage routine, most of the glamor and magic had worn off for me too.

The most overriding aspect of the New York experience though, was the sense of intense energy and vitality that the people and the city exuded. One could feel it in the way New Yorkers were walking, talking, moving. I enjoyed strolling among the shoppers while watching the diversity of people and races, the sound of different accents and languages. To me, there was something special and sensual in the way women dressed and walked. They all seemed to have more beautiful figures, legs, better rhythm and body coordination than European women. I shall, of course, never know whether my observations were based on reality, or whether they were influenced by my state of mind and a determination to view things American in a favorable light. I suspect there was some truth to my perceptions.

IV — LIFE IN TRANSITION

In their immortal *Three Penny Opera*, Weill and Brecht sang:
"Erst kommt das Fressen, und dann kommt die Moral"; (freely
translated: First you must have something to eat, and only then can
you bother with the finer things in life). Because I had been
fortunate to land a job as clerk-secretary at the New York
Lighthouse for the Blind, thanks to Daisy Rogers, I could afford to
eat and reflect on the condition of refugees in New York.

For the time being, I had a steady job at fifteen dollars a week,
enough to get by; the time had come to move away from the
Fourth Reich in Washington Heights towards the center of things.
I found a furnished room in a brownstone rooming house on 62nd
Street between Park and Madison Avenues for a rental of three or
four dollars a week. In 1938 quite a few town houses that formerly
had been privately owned had been converted into rooming houses
as a consequence of the economic situation. They tended to be in
very good, sometimes even elegant sections of the city, and offered
single people a fine opportunity for comfortable quarters. Although
I had to share a bathroom, I enjoyed a quiet view of a little
courtyard with a tree. My new home was just a block and a half
away from my work place which added to my pleasure. The
superintendent helped with getting my belongings downtown in his
jalopy. Things were looking up.

Even though I was now spatially removed from the refugee
centers uptown, I maintained contact with friends and acquaintances from abroad. Those continuing connections helped me to
gain a perspective about particular behaviors of newcomers to this
country, and I hope I was able to learn from this.

I observed that those people who had emigrated at around thirty
or older, had already enjoyed a taste of life as established
professionals in their native countries. They had begun to embark
on careers and some had started families. After a few weeks or

months in their new homeland, the immediate life threat among circumstances that caused them to leave receded into the background, and the bliss of survival against heavy odds began to wear off rather quickly. They now had to face the intimidating task of building, from scratch, a new life in an alien environment and in a foreign language. If they were lucky to find work at all, it was usually at hard menial tasks and they were forced to live in very primitive circumstances, unlike the past experience of many. As a result, they often behaved in a way that was emotionally under- standable, but rationally senseless and bound to appear ungrateful and graceless; they complained and complained, compared notes on how wonderful life had been in the old days, and how bad things were here.

A joke making the rounds in those days illustrated the situation. It seems that two refugee cocker spaniels met at a cafeteria on Broadway. One was nostalgically reminiscing about how he always had eaten steak twice a day in the old country, while the other, wiping a tear off his cheeks, said: "My dear, in Vienna I was a St. Bernard."

Given the human condition, such conduct could be psycho- logically explained, especially in the face of grim realities once the shock effect had subsided, but it could not be condoned easily. Inevitably it antagonized many and caused indignation, resentment and contempt on the part of those who had worked hard to help them. The attitudes of the newcomers were sometimes viewed as arrogant, pompous and lacking in appreciation for the strenuous efforts that were being made on their behalf.

Matters were probably not helped by the fact that most of the current wave of refugees did not quite fit the existing stereotype of previous generations of immigrants. By and large, the present group tended to come from quite sophisticated, middle class backgrounds. Many had been professionally educated; others successful businessmen. Most had a competent command of English. In things American they still were "greenhorns," yet they did not match widely held expectations of what newcomers to these shores would be like.

I determined for myself that I would avoid the caricatured image of the arrogant, ungrateful immigrant. Perhaps the fact that I had not yet any professional achievements to look back on made it easier to feel properly humble and truly grateful.

Yet, I was not spared the hurt and disappointment of over-hearing bigoted, derogatory, often anti-Semitic remarks about the newcomers who were "taking jobs away from native Americans." What a shock it was to find that even here in my promised land, the German-American Bund and its Nazi views had found quite a few admirers.

All over town I ran into newspaper sellers hawking a hate sheet, published by a Catholic priest, Father Coughlin. In its attacks on Jews, it ran a close second to the infamous Nazi journal *Der Stuermer*. At a time when news from abroad became more and more frightening, these slurs touched a very sensitive nerve. I tried not to overestimate the impact on the public at large of the scurrilous lies printed in the *Catholic Worker*; yet, the comments by readers I overheard undermined my hopes and caused me anxiety and sadness.

Because of my name, manner and accent, some people took me for German and projected all the generalizations they had learned to dislike about Germans on me. Remarks delivered in phony exaggerated accents, followed by screams of "Achtung," did not strike me as funny at all. Also, I encountered situations in which my being Jewish became the cause for unflattering generalizations and mockery. Given a choice between two evils, I think I preferred to be hated for being a Jew rather than being mistaken for a German.

Often, those days, the actions of persons or groups caused me great pain, frustration, and, at times fear. Yet, I found it difficult to ascribe those incidents to individual meanness, directed at me personally, even though they resulted in resentment and anger on my part.

There were very few times when anybody expressed antago-nism to me just because I was a refugee and a Jew. Once, during a rehearsal a young woman turned to me and began to unload a stream of anti-foreign, anti-Jewish sentiments. I felt stunned and helpless, almost incapable of defending myself. In my pain, I found no way to respond to her.

In those years preceding Pearl Harbor, my true problems did not come from discrimination, and my complaints were not at all directed at my physical or financial circumstances. On a very deep and emotional level, my life was pervasively overshadowed by a continuing series of Kafkaesque frustrations that met all my efforts to save the lives of my parents. My anguish was compounded by the knowledge that some of the most hurtful of these frustrations could not be blamed on the Nazis. While the Nazis presented the most immediate threat to my parents' survival, the main obstacles that blocked all attempts to rescue them came from the international bureaucracy, more specifically, the United States State Department and Immigration Authorities. The Nazis were willing to let them go at that time. But, neither my parents nor I could find a country that would admit them. All efforts ultimately faltered because of the lack of a visa.

Years later I saw a moving performance of Menotti's *Consul* on Broadway. In a very dramatic and effective way, the play depicted the horrors accompanying endeavors to obtain a refugee visa during that era. It made me appreciate the vast difference that existed between witnessing a theater presentation, even at its best, and actually experiencing the events that were portrayed. It helped me grasp, eventually, the emotional gap that had to exist between what my psychoanalytic patients had lived through and were reporting, and the limits of my empathy.

Even today, more than fifty years later, I can taste the bitterness of defeat and feel the searing pain of my helplessness while the urgency was increasing, and the doors were closing on my parents one by one. Even as I write this, I am almost physically aware of my reluctance, my resistance against recalling and recording the nightmarish sequence of smashed hopes. Yet, I know that I cannot escape from communicating and reliving these events in my attempt to render an honest account of my life and history.

Not unlike Kafka's K, I was not fighting an identifiable enemy.

I knew there was nothing personal about it; there was no conspiracy. Rather, it was the sets of faceless rules and regulations, changing almost daily, that were killing my parents and were dealing deadly blows to me and all my endeavors to save them.

First, there was the matter of getting American citizens of adequate substance to sign "affidavits," guaranteeing that my parents would not ever become financial burdens to the government. Understandably, strangers would not readily think of a foreign banker in his late fifties and his forty- year old opera singer wife, both without any means of support, as good employment risks. As a newcomer to these shores myself, I had only limited access to those who might even consider accepting such legal responsibilities.

Miraculously, it had become possible through the good will of the Ochs family to obtain these documents. As time passed, a glimmer of hope arose that the quickly developing events in Central Europe might lead, on an emergency basis, to a crack in the deadly U.S. quota system. As it was, people born in what was Polish territory after the first world war were locked out for years to come. I fed on rumors that the Roosevelt administration might relax rigid enforcement of quotas for hardship cases.

No sooner did this become a possibility, when there was an administrative change in the requirements for financial disclosures on the part of those who signed affidavits; they were now asked to submit, in great detail, sworn statements about their income, financial transactions and tax declarations. I understood that such regulations could create problems for the Ochs family who had offered help, but who were understandably reluctant to reveal details of their wealth.

While I was exerting all possible efforts to overcome these new difficulties, the State Department issued another ruling. From now on, visas would only be granted if absolute proof could be submitted that transportation to an American port had been obtained and paid for. War had come to Europe in 1939, and boats to the United States left only from Portugal.

I shall spare the reader (and myself) an account of what it took to arrange for passage on a ship scheduled to leave Lisbon for New York. Among other obstacles, a "Catch 22" ploy existed: no visa, no ticket; no ticket, no visa. Finally, the deed was accomplished and we held confirmed reservations.

As war continued to rage in Europe and France fell, the situation of Jews remaining in Vienna became more precarious each day. As it turned out, my parents seemed on the verge of obtaining their American visa, now that they could provide proof of transportation.

One unforgettable afternoon, a telegram arrived, signed by the Fugazy Travel Agency, a name that was forever carved into my memory. It informed me curtly that passage for my parents had been cancelled. No explanation. Inquiries suggested that someone had simply bribed an official at the point of embarkation who gave away the reserved spaces.

I had to start all over again. Mail service continued to operate between Austria, now Germany, and the United States. The *New York Times* published a daily list of departing and arriving ships to and from Europe which made it possible to anticipate when letters might arrive. Usually, it took a week to ten days. While there was reason to suspect that letters would be censored in Vienna, we had worked out simple codes beforehand which would avoid calling the censors' attention to reports of the true state of affairs. The messages became increasingly desperate and urgent.

In November 1938, a Nazi diplomat had been assassinated by a young non-Jewish member of the resistance. The Germans used this occasion to stage as "retaliation" the infamous "Kristallnacht," a pogrom, in the course of which all synagogues in German-ruled territory were destroyed; (broken windows, therefore "crystal night"). With full and official government sanction, Jews were hunted down, some killed, some "arrested," some just beaten up. The international press reported these events, and for the first time, I believe, the world at large was able to comprehend the cruelties and the harbingers of deadly acts of violence that were to follow, and could witness how these were orchestrated. Even by then, rumors about deportations to unknown places, camps in the East, began to make the rounds.

My parents, warned at the last moment, left their apartment and went into hiding. I received a telegram that told me, in our pre-arranged code, that the hour of extreme danger had come, and that flight abroad was a matter of now or never. Yet, this time they survived.

I had spent the evening visiting with a charming and pleasant young woman whom I had been dating. When I came home and heard the news about the infamous Crystal Night, the burning of the synagogues and the hunting down of Jews in Germany and Austria, I was overcome by worry and guilt. How could I enjoy myself and go out on dates while these events affecting my parents were taking place! Right then, on impulse, I sat down and wrote a note ending this relationship.

One didn't have to be paranoid to suspect that there were forces within the U.S. government that were less than enthusiastic about rushing to the rescue of the increasingly desperate victims of Nazi persecution. Odd as this may seem, a straining of relationships between Germany and the United States led to another, and this time fatal, obstacle that blocked my parents' rescue.

The invasion of Poland in 1939 and the outbreak of fighting in Europe led to increased diplomatic tension between Washington and Berlin. At some point, the American government decided to close all its consulates in Germany and in the territories she occupied. While this vividly demonstrated U.S. disapproval of the Nazi regime, it also removed with one stroke any opportunity for potential immigrants to receive their visa. In effect, even though you may have obtained an affidavit, a quota number and passage, and even a German passport with the word JEW stamped across it, now there was no American Consulate within reach to issue the visa that had been approved.

Yet, there was a way to get around these new difficulties. All it took was money. Apparently, it was possible to make an arrangement with the government of Cuba. What was required, as I recall, was one thousand dollars in cash per person for miscellaneous "fees"; in addition a bond in the amount of four or five thousand dollars had to be posted for each person. The bond money was to be returned once the U.S. visa was obtained from the American Consul in Havana, and the refugee would presumably be on his or her way to the United States.

It all seems like a simple, straightforward arrangement. But, it took money and I had none. For months I knocked on every door I could find, pleaded, begged, cajoled, with no success. Some friends, some of them refugees themselves, helped me to scratch together loans that could have paid for the cash fees, but the bond money proved elusive, no matter how hard I tried.

Most dramatically, perhaps, I felt hurt and disappointed when my new wife's millionaire uncle refused to help me put up a bond that could have saved the life of my parents. It seemed easy to find reasonable causes. There was a depression on. Did "Uncle Walter" know enough about me to trust me?

I did not want to hate, I consciously wanted to escape self-pity, self-doubt and anything that would enhance hopelessness. I did not always succeed in maintaining full self-confidence, but, I suspect that, when reality did not quite fit my conscious purpose I was not beyond twisting and changing facts in my mind to fit my purpose.

I learned something significant about myself during those days of agony and hopelessness. The situation I found myself in made me test how far to the edge I could go. I even considered holding up a bank; it was, after all, a question of life or death for the two people dearest to me in the entire world. I knew I couldn't do that. At the risk of being accused of deceiving myself, I am convinced that my reasons were not related to cowardice and fear. I just knew that there were boundaries I could not cross.

A similar moment occurred years later when, as an American GI, I found myself in charge of German Africa Corps prisoners, on the very day that I had received definite confirmation of my parents' death in Auschwitz. I thought that I could or even should, grab a gun and shoot some of the Germans who represented the murderers of my parents. For better or worse, I faltered. I did not have the capacity for such impulsive, violent action.

Not knowing where else to turn for the bond money, I

remembered in my despair the kind Irish judge from Cleveland whom I had met on board ship while crossing the Atlantic, and who had volunteered to sign affidavits for some of my friends. I wrote him, describing my situation. To my extreme delight and eternal gratitude, he responded by return mail. Yes, he would be glad to help and would post the required bond, provided the National Refugee Service would verify the conditions.

No words could adequately describe my relief and excitement. All letters and documents were arranged as swiftly as possible and, on December 5, 1941, I was advised that my parents would be granted a visa to enter Cuba. On December 7, the Japanese attacked Pearl Harbor, we were at war, and all hopes to save my parents came to an end.

Could I have rescued them? Could I have acted with more determination, greater speed, more resourcefulness? I shall never know, even though the feeling persists that I *should* have been more effective. As I recall these events, everything else that happened in those years preceding Pearl Harbor pales and fades into a haze of irrelevance. Yet, such is the thrust for survival and the power of denial that I was able to continue the daily routine of managing my life.

I really understood the resilience the human mind and body could muster under stress. I saw the role our defense mechanisms can play when they enable us to carry on when things around us seem to crumble. Of course, there was a price to pay. Eventually, it took a lot of work and time to try to unravel the neurotic patterns that were acquired or reinforced then, but they served their purpose.

Four years later, I received a letter from my friend George whose unit was stationed with the American forces in Europe. He had gone to Theresienstadt and had dug up some of the relevant documents, confirming my worst fears. The Germans were thorough archivists, and I learned in some detail of my parents' deportation to Theresienstadt, their stay there, and their subsequent transport to their death in Auschwitz in October of 1944. George wrote: "Trite as it may sound, remember the old inscription 'This too shall pass'." And pass it did. I continued to live, to function and to struggle. Feelings of guilt and lingering pain were submerged and not allowed to haunt and overwhelm me.

Many years later, during a visit to Israel, my wife and I visited the Holocaust Museum in Jerusalem. A peculiar thing happened. We felt sad as we entered the hall where large slabs of stone marked the names of the various extermination camps; I believe it was called "The Hall of Remembrance." Suddenly, I was sobbing uncontrollably, and for the next half hour or so, I was unable to stop. My wife, Marie held me as I struggled to regain some control. When I finally succeeded, I experienced an extraordinary sense of relief as we walked out into the sunshine of Jerusalem. And again, five years later, in Jerusalem, almost out of curiosity, I felt the need to test myself, and so again we went to Yad Vashem, the Holocaust Museum. This time I thought I would observe, be detached, as I entered the Hall of Remembrance calmly. Within seconds, I was again helplessly clutched by spasms of deep sobs that I could not restrain for almost an hour until, much later, a taxi brought us back to our hotel. I had tapped reserve pools of sorrow and agony deep within me that were ready to spurt out beyond conscious control in this environment.

The message that the possession of a passport and/or visa could make the difference between life and death left a deep imprint. The establishment of the State of Israel acquired a special meaning for me. I, never a nationalist, or a Zionist, for that matter, was deeply affected by the existence of a sovereign Jewish entity, a nation, a state, able to create laws that allowed any Jew in the entire world who was being persecuted to apply for and obtain a passport, citizenship and asylum. I, never a militarist, having known and seen Jews to be the defenseless victims of armed thugs, was moved to tears by the sight of armed Jewish soldiers, men and women, marching smartly by.

V — AMERICANIZATION AND ROMANCE

In the years before the war, a number of my contemporaries and friends from Vienna began to appear in New York. We all wanted to become Americanized as soon and as completely as possible. However, our common background, the similarity of our situation, our loneliness in an alien land, the history of our past affection for each other, all exerted a strong pull. So, while we insisted on talking to each other in English, we were drawn together, took walks, hiked in the New Jersey Palisades, ate together occasionally, and lent each other moral support.

My main concern was to try and blend in as much as I could. My father's friend, the Vienna correspondent of the *New York Times*, had half-jokingly counseled me before my departure: "If you want to get along in America, always keep your shoes shined, your cheeks cleanly shaven, have your hair cut regularly, and never, never, even if you should be one, call yourself an atheist or a Communist." I found it easy and useful to follow these guidelines.

I learned to eat the "American way," switching my fork to the right hand after cutting food, abandoning the European habit of keeping the fork in the left hand. I took my hat off in elevators, tipped my hat to ladies only after they had acknowledged me, and only when I wanted to demonstrate an odd Viennese custom, did I bend to kiss a lady's hand.

In spite of my loneliness and desire to date, my involvements with women were limited to a few short affairs. Some were with friends from Europe; some with young women I met in New York. All of them were superficial. They satisfied some needs and some curiosity, and nobody was much hurt when they broke off. I was not ready to enter into any more lasting relationships.

It took a while to understand the cultural differences between the dating practices of young people in Vienna, and those prevalent in New York. World War I had disrupted many of the traditions that had governed the relationships between men and women in Europe. Much like the situation in America after World War II, a sort of sexual revolution had taken place a few years earlier.

I did not find it easy to understand the oxymoron of a mixture of easy camaraderie and apparent sexual constriction. In the light of my past experiences I had trouble with the then publicly accepted view that sexual intimacy was something that men were after and women would reluctantly grant given the proper inducements. The importance of money spent on a date, the role assigned to the intake of alcohol, the seemingly great value placed on women's chastity and virginity, the clear cut divisions made between "nice" and "easy" girls; all that was very puzzling and took a while to absorb. So did the concept of "pure" versus "sullied" girls. I realized even then that the rules were not always as strictly enforced as they were pronounced; yet, a man was expected to know them and to act accordingly. These norms were shared by everybody who grew up here, and I was expected to conform to them.

Dinner invitations, stemming from my letters of recommendation continued. At one of these in August 1939, I was introduced to an interesting Dutch designer, Elsa, who had come to this country not long before. She lived a few blocks away from me. While it was clear that we were not attracted to each other, we enjoyed each other's company, and spent time together as friends.

One night, after Elsa and I had dinner together, she invited me to come up to her apartment where she had arranged to meet a woman friend. Marie Louise became my wife in 1941 about two years later, and we are still married.

The woman I saw was slender, 5 foot 6, about 105 pounds, with brown hair and gentle brown eyes set in a pretty, oval face with a friendly expression that seemed to signal: "Show me." I thought she had a lovely figure and a fawn-like demeanor, which I found very attractive.

Beyond the immediate attraction we both felt for each other, several factors brought us closer and closer together. Marie was a native New Yorker from a background somewhat similar to mine. She had gone to school in Lausanne, Switzerland, and had been on her way to medical school when the great depression canceled those aspirations. The years she had spent in Europe helped create a bond of understanding between us. She had a brief, unsuccessful marriage that had been dissolved, even before a son, Andy, was born. We often joked that what really brought us together was that she lived less than a five-minute walk away from my house. I am still being teased today about my sexual aggressiveness at those early meetings.

We saw each other more and more often, my other friends and she got along, and, we soon became steady companions. We had our share of arguments and spats, (still have,) but we managed to survive them together. An electric coffeemaker that Marie had given me once became the symbol of our tiffs and reconciliations. When we had a fight I returned it to her; when we reconciled, she brought it to my house.

Although I did not feel ready then to think of permanent involvements, Marie began to fill an empty space in my life that I had not even allowed myself to know was there. There was and is about her a quiet gentleness which hides a well of powerful inner strength and determination, as well as a fine artistic talent that she expressed much later in life through her art work. Under stress she comes through. One time I was in the living room when I heard her call calmly and matter-of-factly: "Fred, there is a fire in the kitchen!" There was, and she was in the process of putting it out.

While being quite undemanding in material things, she provided, beyond love and caring, steady and loyal emotional support and encouragement. She had lived through difficult times and was able to understand me and to feel with me when I was in need. Increasingly, we shared good times and bad. I suspect that secretly she saw herself, and perhaps I saw her a little that way too, as filling in for my mother, and protecting me.

As time went on, I could not imagine life without Marie. In the spring of 1941, I innocently bought a ring for her birthday, and lo, we were engaged. In August of that year we decided we might just as well make it legal, and so we did. Neither of us had any money, but we felt that we might just as well be poor and venturesome together.

In my mind there were lots of questions, hesitations and doubts. Was I ready to make a commitment for life? Was I compromising my sacred responsibility to look after my parents above anything else; was I betraying my duty to dedicate all my available energies and resources to saving them? Was I mature enough to be a stepfather to Andy?

Somehow, I found answers that allowed me to overcome my fears. On what seemed sound intellectual and emotional grounds, I made the decision to plunge ahead, albeit, I must confess, at moments with my eyes tightly shut.

The appointed time for our wedding arrived. I had taken a couple of days off from my singing duties at a hotel in the Catskills, and presented myself that morning at the apartment Marie and Andy shared with her parents, ready for whatever might follow.

There I found my closest childhood friend, George, then living in Chicago, whom I had asked to be my best man. He had arrived early in the morning of that day. My future father-in-law, finding a stranger in the living room with Marie in the morning exclaimed: "For heaven's sake, has she changed her mind again?" She had not, and so we all shared a car ride to Greenwich, Connecticut, where we met the rest of our small wedding party, and appeared, as previously arranged, before a Justice of the Peace.

George, a musician and budding conductor and I had been close friends for a very long time. In fact, Marie claims that she first learned about our wedding plans when I mentioned that I had written to George asking him to be my best man. In the past, he and I had often bounced musical passages off each other. Quite innocently, in honor of old times, we did the same on the trip to the wedding. Marie has never forgiven me for having chanted Verdi's Requiem Mass all the way up to Greenwich.

When we finally got there, I slipped the Justice of the Peace a ten dollar bill, as I had been told was the custom. I did not know Marie's father had done the same. As a result, we were subjected to an especially lengthy discourse on the blessings of observing the golden rule; Marie and I became quite giggly and had a terrible time keeping our faces straight.

Then, it was done. Marie's parents hosted a lovely wedding luncheon for a small group of friends, and I participated in the party as a married man. For the rest of the day, George, who had come all the way from Chicago just for that day, did not leave us out of his sight for one moment. When we finally retired to the honeymoon suite which my parents-in-law had arranged at the Hotel Dorset, George came up with us on the elevator and it took a very emphatic "Good night, George!" from Marie to permit us privacy on our wedding night.

VI — THE JOY OF SINGING

After about a year and a half, my secretarial job at the N.Y. Lighthouse for the Blind ended. Perhaps my superiors sensed that my heart was not fully in the clerical tasks assigned to me. They were probably quite right. Yet, I am grateful for the opportunities the regular income gave me. I was able to gain a foothold in America, to work on my aspirations for a singing career and to learn more of what life here was all about. Probably, some of the time I spent on catnaps in the bathroom of the Lighthouse helped regain my alertness, but they did not go unnoticed and speeded up my departure.

While I was still working there, I was sent on an errand to deliver something to the Butler Library at Columbia University. Here I was, a messenger boy, looking at the heady atmosphere of the campus, the hallowed buildings, the young people engrossed in books or in discussions. A wave of yearning and sadness came over me, and a sense of despair that I could not be with them; that their world would, in all likelihood, be forever closed to me. In 1958, when I received my Ph.D. at Columbia University I recalled that day vividly.

I also learned from my experience of being fired, for the second time since my arrival, that employment was quite different from Austria. There, a job like my father's, for example, implied a life-long career with one employer. To lose it suggested failure and could present a serious threat to economic survival. Here, on the other hand, changing jobs or being fired, while never pleasant, was part of mobility and apparently an experience not unique to me, but shared by many Americans.

Around that time my vocal teacher considered me ready to try for some singing engagements, and try I did. At the same time I searched for secretarial work where I hoped my linguistic abilities could be of some use. And so I began the rounds of auditions for church, temple and show jobs.

Two agents supplied soloists and quartet members to the various churches and temples in the Metropolitan area: Jimmy Price at Steinway Hall and Catherine Carey at Carnegie Hall. Both were pleasant, decent people. Once you were on their file, you could stop by as often as you wished to inquire about jobs. As the supply of singers exceeded the demand, the agents did not call unless they were truly stuck. Fees for these engagements ranged from a normal five dollars to a rare maximum of twenty five. Carey and Price, depending on a tiny commission for their livelihood, had to strive for volume and could not afford to waste time.

Vocally and technically, I apparently qualified for the jobs they had to offer, but I had some obstacles to overcome. My sight-reading skills were not up to the phenomenally high standards of American-trained singers. Diction was also a problem. Protestant churches, especially, were concerned about accents and foreign sounds. For instance, as I had studied English with a British teacher, it took me a while to learn to sing "Israyel" rather than "Isr-ael", and "Aybraham" instead of "Ahbraham", "ahgen" rather than "agayn."

I had a repertoire of oratorio arias, but the custom then was to use "Sacred Solos" during church services. This required additional preparation. Most of these songs were written by composers around the turn of the century to psalm texts or occasional poetic religious improvisations. Musically, they tended to be bombastic, empty, occasionally quoting one or two phrases from classic oratorios. They held a Victorian, nostalgic popular appeal for older parishioners. I hated these songs fervently. I even thought of them as blasphemous, but, once again, I allowed my survival needs to triumph, and I accommodated. I really loved singing "A mighty fortress.."and" God of our fathers..."

Lastly, my name with its "Jewish" connotation was not always deemed to be helpful in introducing me to certain music directors or organists. In the interest of "survival" I did not protest if the card of introduction managed to misspell my name and, sometimes, I became the Bass Fred Hackett or Hatch. For better or worse, I was too poor to be proud.

Eventually, these hurdles were overcome and I joined the many aspiring young New York singers who survived by taking "church and temple jobs." There were additional advantages. I studied, deepened my repertoire, and used my voice in performances. Exposure to different faiths, denominations, rituals, organists, and choir conductors expanded my knowledge of the various sub-groups in the New York community. I met, and occasionally became friends with, other singers and exchanged information with them on open jobs, auditions, and general music gossip.

The singers for the most part had excellent voices. In many churches and temples the choir sang from the choir loft and was hidden by a screen from the congregation. During sermons which we could barely hear anyway, I enriched my supply of jokes substantially. I found that the professional singers who participated in the services, not unlike myself, were almost always only involved religiously when they were singing a solo. For the rest of the time, by and large, they were respectfully doing the professional job they were paid to do.

In the end, I landed a permanent job in the choir of Temple Emanu-El, the oldest and largest Jewish Reform Temple in New York. While the pay was just as low as it was in all other such engagements, this one was steady work.

At that time I was living on East 83rd Street, around the corner from the Roman Catholic Church Ignatius de Loyola. Their organist and music director was a specialist on Gregorian Chant and taught me to admire and love some of that literature. As my back window faced the back windows of the church's parish house, it was simple for them to summon me on a moment's notice for a requiem that required a sung liturgy. All they did was wave a handkerchief at me through their back window, and I gratefully earned an extra five dollars.

Another field of employment for aspiring singers, including those with classical rather than pop music ambitions, was in the area of "club dates" and what had become known as the "Borscht Belt." Borscht Circuit Hotels, so named after "Borscht," a beet soup and a Russian-Jewish favorite, were the many inns that had sprung up in the Catskill Mountains within about 100 miles of New York. For relatively low cost, they offered fresh air, lakes, simple lodgings, notoriously large amounts of mostly kosher food, and entertainment to their predominantly Jewish clientele. The accommodations ranged from very small unpretentious camps to the palatial splendors of the famous Grossinger, Concord, Nevele and such. Even the very smallest of them had a "casino" for the after dinner entertainment of their guests.

At their best, these hotels offered a fertile training ground for some of the future top personalities in American entertainment. Milton Berle, Danny Kaye and Robert Merrill were among the stars that developed their art there.

At their worst, they were dreadfully exploitive of their help and catered to the lowest level of taste. The agents who booked these shows worked from little cubbyholes around Broadway and Seventh Avenue, between 46th and 52nd Street. Usually they were survivors of the bygone great era of vaudeville.

After my initial painful experiences, I learned that I was expected to sing four to six numbers, possibly participate in a "blackout sketch" and join in an opening and finale. But that was much, much later.

My first assignment came from an agent for whom I had auditioned by singing eight bars of the Toreador song, without accompaniment, in his office. It was the start of the summer season. I received a bus ticket and was given the name and telephone number of the hotel and its owner. I also was promised an unbelievably low salary (even for those times) for the summer, and was assured that food and lodging would be on the house.

This was at the beginning of my second year in America. My musical experience, even as a listener, had consisted of concert repertoire, opera, perhaps an operetta, some movie musicals, and a few pop tunes I had heard on the radio. I was prepared to sing things like "Ole Man River," "Road to Mandalay," some Cole Porter, Gershwin and operatic arias.

On arrival at the resort, I found out that I was the entire

entertainment staff. I was expected to be Master of Ceremonies, tell jokes, sing, and, with the help of waiters and busboys, stage short skits and involve the guests in "amateur shows" which I was to produce.

Next, came three days of pure undiluted hell that tested every bit of nerve I could ever muster, as I tried to survive in front of an audience that screamed: "Sing Pagliacci!" (Why should they be expected to know that the aria they meant was written for a tenor and I was a baritone?) Management and I agreed on a bus ticket back to New York. Broke, but immensely relieved, I chalked it all up to experience.

Soon, our financial resources approached a precarious level. Marie had taken a sales job at a department store, and I auditioned for anybody who would listen to me, but our money was about to run out. I was sustained by a firm faith in Hecht's law of personal gravity which stated that all things that came down must come up again; we just hoped it would happen soon; very soon.

Quite often, I did not get the jobs I hoped for, and there was no shortage of rejections. The "cattle calls" when several hundred singers lined up to audition for a few openings in a show were humiliating, degrading events. Inevitably, the producers, directors and conductors who sat in a darkened theater while the applicants paraded in front of them seemed to me arrogant and condescending. The auditioning singers all wanted something desperately, and the listeners just wanted to get it over with as fast as possible. The "thank you," which often followed three bars of singing, cut icily through my hopes and always made me question my worth and talent.

I tried to be brutally honest in assessing my appearance. I was six feet tall and weighed about 200 pounds; blue eyes; brown hair. I had a tendency to look slightly overweight, very slightly, I hoped. Face seemed OK. All told, not too bad, I decided.

What kept me from bitterness, I believe, was, an at least intellectual appreciation of the state of mind of those who made me feel so bad. I readily allowed that I might not be the type they were looking for, my accent might be wrong, I could be too heavy, or too tall, my voice might be too classical, and so on. Once I could find a reasonable cause, I was spared the odious feelings of anger and rage. Considering my past, it was very important, if not always easy, to hold on to some respect for myself. The audition process, by its nature, exposed self-esteem to constant battering.

But then, it happened! I had auditioned for a famous Broadway conductor, Lehman Engel, a wonderful musician and nice person. He offered me a contract for a Broadway show that was scheduled to go into rehearsal three weeks later.

Ah, the dreams of glitz and glamor! Not only would I be paid the then impressive sum of forty dollars a week, but I would be able, in fact, be required, to join Actors' Equity. Membership in the union would place me among the professionals who had priority on all casting calls and who were paid, at the least, union minimum. The show, significantly, was called *Heavenly Express*, and was produced by the prestigious Group Theater. It starred the famous Jules (John) Garfield.

I truly felt in heaven and could not wait to tell Marie and to celebrate this wonderful happening. Singing eight times a week in a Broadway show was not the fulfillment of my dreams, which remained to star in opera and concert. But performing on a real theater stage, becoming part of professional theater, and, earning regular income, exhilarated me.

I suppose I was preoccupied with money before all other considerations. Without financial resources, facing responsibilities that I could not discharge without money, and lacking a familial support system, income became like food for a starving person. I do not think I was greedy; I could hardly afford to be, but I learned that money, when badly needed and not available, became dominant in one's mind and actions.

So we celebrated, even borrowed some money, and basked in the prospect of entering the life of show business. As the day of the first rehearsal approached my anxiety rose; but when I met the three other singers who were the musical backup for what was planned as a straight play, pleasant excitement took over. We rehearsed at Lehman Engel's comfortable apartment as we read through the musical manuscript. It was all quite wonderful, and I remember vividly that Lehman, after we finished rehearsing, played a new recording for us that he had just received. It was Billie Holiday singing "Strange Fruit," a stirring ballad about the lynching and hanging of a black man in the "gallant South."

What I did not know was that all Equity contracts at that time contained a clause permitting the producers to cancel any agreement during the first three days of rehearsal without having to compensate the actors. The Group Theater decided on the third day that it would be more economical to record the music and play it back stage rather than employ live singers. So we cut a record, I collected forty dollars, and the first part of my Broadway dream came to a swift and not very encouraging end.

I admit to some satisfaction when I learned later that the show had opened in Washington to bad reviews and closed three days later. With some bitterness I learned an important lesson about illusions and show business.

A "funny" story was making the rounds in those days: A starving actor had just landed a wonderful part in a Broadway show. As the third day of rehearsals arrived, he felt more and more panicked. When he arrived home at the end of the rehearsal day, he paced up and down and regaled his roommate with stories about how the director had looked at him critically. He knew that the producer had until midnight to fire him without pay and felt certain that he was about to be dumped. At 11:57 the doorbell rang at the front door of his rooming house. Terror stricken, he ran downstairs, flung open the door and saw a Western Union messenger. As he tore open the telegram, an expression of bliss came on his face. "Thank God," he exclaimed, "Aunt Millie has died." I could understand how he might have felt.

Yet, the best was yet to come. Somehow, we muddled through the hard times, searching for any available job, while continuing voice and repertoire studies. Before long a real Broadway show came along. I auditioned successfully for Maestro Maurice Abravanell, a conductor of world renown who was the music director of a new show for which Kurt Weill, the composer of the *Three Penny Opera*, had written the music. The book was by Moss Hart, the lyrics by Ira Gershwin, and the title of the show was *Lady in the Dark*. For whatever mystical significance this may have held for my future life, the subject of the show was the psychoanalysis of an overwrought woman editor.

The show opens in an analyst's office as a straight play. Whenever the heroine describes a dream, music begins, and in seconds, the revolving stages turn the office into a colorful musical scene. It was a wonderful idea, the cast was absolutely top layer, and the show became a smash success. The English actress Gertrude Lawrence played the editor, McDonald Carey and Victor Mature, Danny Kaye and Bert Litell had supporting roles. Singers were carefully chosen and given solo passages. Quite a few of them later went on to successful careers in concert and opera.

This time I survived the third day terrors, and experienced all the excitement that I had anticipated in the previous show adventure. Everything about *Lady in the Dark* was glamorous. Rehearsals took place on the real stage of a Broadway theater; the rehearsal pianist was a superb artist; the music was thrilling; Abravanell was a joy to work with. The morale of the cast was extremely high, and everybody seemed friendly and interested in each other. These were intoxicating weeks, preceding the Boston opening.

All the experiences were stimulating, new and challenging. Some of the most outstanding memories I have are about watching Gertrude Lawrence begin to rehearse the "Ballad of Jenny," a piece that became legendary, and of choreographer Albertina Rasch trying to teach Lawrence some steps. Lawrence, usually unflappable, became more and more irritable and nervous. With her straight acting background, she had concerns about her singing voice. This culminated in a confrontation and shouting match with Rasch which was memorable. All was quickly patched up, and, at the opening, Lawrence stopped the show with her "Ballad of Jenny" for what seemed a full half hour.

I had a short dancing sequence with her. She had a wonderful sense of humor and enlivened matters at some rehearsals by dancing quite seductively with this very young and very green singer. I gladly admit to a small crush on this glamorous woman. She had an air of playfulness about her that invited a sense of intimacy. Feeling the closeness and the heat of her body, acknowledging her inviting smile caused a mixture of arousing, yet embarrassing, sensations. This beautiful woman, the "star," seemed to be sending signals of erotic interest my way which my body readily acknowledged. Yet, I always felt that she was very sure about who she was and that she found it easy to establish the social distance she desired at any given time without her having to say or do anything. It felt exciting to spend time around her, observe her at work, and to feel part of her circle. Inevitably, she inspired extensive and pleasurable fantasies. It was easy to deal with the fact that they were doomed to remain just that.

Rehearsals were followed by the trip to Boston, the parties, the opening night. I marveled as Danny Kaye did his famous "I Love Russian Composers" number, in which he rattled off what seemed like hundreds of names of Russian composers in three or so minutes and stopped the show to a roar of applause. As he came off stage, he ran into me; I congratulated him; he looked crestfallen and said "I'm through, they'll never let me stop the show four minutes before Gertrude Lawrence's big 'Ballad of Jenny.'" As it turned out, Lawrence went on and stopped the show as well, perhaps even for a few seconds longer. The next day, Danny Kaye's salary was doubled and he was transformed from a promising Borscht Circuit comedian into a luminous stage personality.

Contrary to some published reports, I found that Danny Kaye displayed a charming sense of humor off stage. He was easy to talk to, allowed himself to share concerns, kidded around a lot, and flirted playfully with the women backstage. There was no hint that he was not getting along well with Sylvia Fine, his wife, who was writing a good deal of his comedy material. Throughout, I saw no indication whatsoever of his rumored bisexuality.

When he spoke to Marie, then my fiancée, who came backstage

occasionally, he teased her by warning her not to marry me. "He is always the last out after the show. Beware of men who take long to get dressed." Before I went into the Army, I visited him in his dressing room at the Paramount Theater where he was appearing. I fondly remember his warmth as he wished me well.

Gertrude Lawrence was an extraordinary star to work with. She exhausted herself so much on stage that, during the early part of the run, she went to a hospital after each evening show to rest until the next performance. She was a woman of great generosity. When a member of the cast died, early during the run, Lawrence took care of all expenses related to his burial. Christmas 1940, before the show came into New York, all cast members received a letter from her informing them that a sum of money had been donated in their name to British War Relief. Lawrence, a patriotic English-woman, felt that during these serious times a donation in lieu of a Christmas present was appropriate. I still cherish my letter.

The day after the New York opening at the Alvin Theater, when all the glowing reviews had been published and heard, Moss Hart, who had also directed the show, came to the dressing room and said: "Folks, we now can send out the laundry!"

The Boston "tryout" gave me my first glance at another Ameri-can city. It was not until the early fifties, when I appeared with the New England Opera Theater, that I realized what a narrow and un-representative aspect of Boston I had come to know then. All activities were centered on the area where the theater was located. At first, most of my time was spent at the Colonial Theater, where the frantic rehearsals and dress rehearsals preceding the opening night took place, and where we worked on the changes and modifications made after the debut. The hotel was located not far from the theater.

In contrast to the thrills and excitement on stage, this time was somewhat grim for me. Life consisted of rehearsals, performing, and elaborate planning for dinner outings with other members of the cast. Our free time was spent on some sightseeing, walking in the Commons and on Beacon Hill braving the New England winds, or visiting the somewhat seedy nightclub area in the vicinity of the

Colonial Theater.

A delightful tradition permitted cast members in town to attend any other theater, movie or vaudeville house as a complimentary guest. We spent the rest of our free time relaxing in well-heated theaters, watching other show people at work.

This was the winter of 1940 and 1941. War was on the horizon, and Boston was a Navy town. Blue laws ordained that no alcoholic beverages could be served after midnight on Saturdays. Sailors would order huge amounts of liquor just before curfew and on Sunday mornings we watched from our windows as ambulances and Armed Forces Police picked up the drunks from the icy gutters. The cold was penetrating and, in the absence of local friends and acquaintances, the city did not seem very inviting.

Toward the end of 1942, when I played the Schubert Theater nearby in the *Ziegfeld Follies of 1943*, starring Milton Berle, I felt the same way about winters in the theater section of Boston. By that time the war had started and I had been married for more than a year.

Shortly before the Boston tryout, Marie's brother, who was part of a gun crew on a merchant ship, made port there. He escorted some dates to what was then a fashionable night club, the *Coconut Grove*, not far from the theater. A horrendous fire erupted that night, and more than six hundred people tragically burned to death. A large part of Harry's body surface was destroyed, but he survived, and was able to pick up his life after undergoing about two years of hospitalization and rehabilitation. Walking through the dirty, white, cold streets of that part of the city, and smelling even a year later the residual odor of fire and smoke, I felt an aura of terror that cast a pall over those old memories of Boston.

While Marie and I had spent almost all our free time together in New York, in 1940 we were not yet married, and, in the midst of all the theatrical excitement, I felt quite lonely, although everybody in the cast was friendly and accepting. Several of the people I spent most of my time with came from various parts of the South, West and the Middle West. I discovered that they came from backgrounds and value systems very different not only from mine, but even from those I had come to know and expect from my fellow New Yorkers. On issues of race, politics, or unions, for example, they must have thought of me as a dangerous radical, while I did not appreciate what appeared to me to be their ultra-conservative positions and seeming disregard for the poor and powerless. Although we got along and even socialized, I felt very alien, and was glad to return to the more familiar surroundings of the Big Apple.

Once settled into a successful New York run, every show has to cope with the problem of keeping the cast alert and on edge, so that the staleness that can come from performing the same roles week after week can be avoided. Danny Kaye made an unforgettable contribution to this situation.

In the last dream sequence, the "circus dream," he had his back to the audience while the entire cast faced forward. Gertrude Lawrence, in front of him, was voicing her conflict about which cover to select for the spring issue of her magazine by shouting dramatically to the audience: "The Eastercover, The Circus-cover?!" while Danny, in the nondream- part her art director, in the dream a ringmaster, held up one after the other of the cover mockups from which she had to choose.

The problem for all of us, including Gertrude, was that we, and she, were watching his face, which the audience could not see. He mugged and distorted his features as only Danny Kaye could, and it took every effort we were able to muster not to break into uncontrollable laughter. The contest between Danny and the rest of us, frowned on by the disapproving stage manager, kept things at very high tension. I had never before realized how difficult it was to keep from losing control when one stood on stage, in front of the public, in the required state of heightened alertness.

After we opened and became a "hit" in New York, things settled down to a regular routine. With the exception of an occasional rehearsal, there were just eight shows a week (two matinees and Sundays off), a small but regular income, and time to pursue further steps toward a career in classical music. The show experience strengthened my yearning to do what I could to ready myself for a concert and opera career. I enjoyed my work on Broadway, but I also knew that it was and always would be only a means to an end for me.

Life outside the theater went on. The struggle to save my parents' lives continued. With every day that passed, it became more obvious that only a short time remained before the United States would enter the war. In one way I looked forward desperately to the time when the seemingly invincible Nazi forces would finally encounter a power that, I hoped, would bring them to their knees. But I was also frightened of all the unpredictable events that the future could bring, how it would affect my parents, my life, and the course of history.

I had grown up in the shadow of World War I; the anti-war literature of that period, represented by books like *All Quiet on the Western Front* profoundly shaped my attitudes to war as a way of settling the problems of the world. I despised and feared the senseless brutalities and cruel blood baths that were part of war. I had listened to the war stories my uncle and others told about their military service in combat. Yet, here was this monster, Hitler, threatening to engulf the world and those closest to me; clearly nothing but brute force could stop him. Sooner or later, I knew my draft number would be up and I would have to participate actively in these events. I also knew, and this with mixed feelings, that I would not volunteer before I was called.

In the course of my life, I had acquired significant experience in suppressing what I did not want to interfere with the progress of daily events. For better or for worse, my defenses came into play, and helped me to continue to concentrate on my job, plans for my career and soon, on marriage.

Some chances to get my feet wet as a solo performer on radio and in recitals surfaced. None of these appearances were paid, but they presented opportunities for practice and experience. New York's classic music station WQXR engaged me for a concert; so did WNYC, New York's Municipal Station, where I was a soloist with the WNYC orchestra; I participated in a student recital at the

New York College of Music and in other such public performances. Usually, I sang a few operatic arias and a variety of art
songs and Lieder. Reactions were all favorable and a number of
appreciative letters encouraged me to take advantage of an offer to
give a solo concert recital of my own at the Friendship House on
Park Avenue and 85th Street.

With the help of my friend and accompanist, Otto Gruenbaum,
I prepared a full length program which was well attended and
enthusiastically received. Gruenbaum, as an American soldier, died
in the last days of World War II while on his way to visit Richard
Strauss in Bavaria. His body and jeep were not found until after the
spring thaw. No information was ever available concerning the circumstances of his death, whether by sniper bullet or road accident.

By the summer, I felt ready to again attempt a summer in the
Catskills, the Borscht Circuit. This time I was a member of an
entertainment team at a large hotel, and my responsibilities were
limited. I sang in the shows and participated in skits, openings and
finales. On days off, I went to New York to prepare for my impending "nuptials." Although this work gave me welcome performing experience, I still felt like a fish out of water, and disliked
the entire scene.

Then came my "operatic debut." The "Popular Price Grand
Opera Company" performed standard repertoire on Saturday
nights at the Brooklyn Academy. The impresario, a well known
character with very long, very black hair and a heavy Italian
accent, known as "The Maestro," prided himself on his knowledge
of voices, and he was able to produce opera performances with
orchestra, sets and costumes for a modest admission price. He
usually managed to engage a few operatic stars on their way down
for the leading roles, and employed youngsters such as me for
supporting parts. After he heard my audition, he offered me my
"debut" as the King in Verdi's *Aida*.

When I appeared for rehearsal, I found to my consternation that
I was the only singer there. The stage director informed me: "You
come in here, and you exit there." The conductor said: "Just watch
me!" That was the end of "the rehearsal."

I joined the American Guild of Musical Artists, the union representing classical musicians, and appeared in time for the performance. Some of my more experienced colleagues helped me get into my costume and apply the elaborate makeup of an Egyptian king. I entered where I had been told and exited at the right place. Everything went swimmingly until the ballet came on. I was sitting on my throne next to my "daughter" Amneris, staring into space as I had seen other Egyptian pharaohs do in pictures, when the full house exploded into loud laughter. Convinced that my false beard must have started to descend, I whispered to Amneris: "What the hell is going on?" and she whispered back that the ballet girl in bra and panties performing in front of me had just lost her bra.

Apparently my debut was successful because I was quickly re-engaged, and even offered a new part, Count Monterone in *Rigoletto*, a role in which I made my debut with the New York City Opera seven years later. Back then, I learned whether I was scheduled to sing the next Saturday by seeing my name listed in the cast announcements that the New York Times published on preceding Sundays.

Payment followed an interesting ritual. Just before the curtain rose, a union representative sitting at a table backstage handed out pay envelopes. As agreed, I would find the minimum union pay, $10, in the envelope. On the way back to the dressing room, "Maestro," the producer, stood with outstretched hand to collect his kickback of five dollars. You either followed the ritual or you stopped singing with his company.

Who could forget "Maestro's" impassioned appeal to the audience's patriotism on the Saturday following Pearl Harbor? Before the curtain went up, he stepped in front of it, spoke of his love for his adopted country, and finished by announcing: "I want you to know that my son, the tenor without a voice, is in the Philippines!"

The first *Rigoletto* with the Brooklyn Company was memorable for another reason. The costume for Count Monterone was clearly made for somebody much slimmer than myself. As there was no fitting, I discovered thirty minutes before curtain time that I could not squeeze into the costume. I can still feel my heart pounding as I think back to four people trying to pin me into pants while I listened to the opening chords of the opera and knew that I was due on stage in minutes. Somehow I made it.

The costume was black. Marie, who had been trying for some time to get me to lose some weight, likes to tell the story about an Italian lady who was sitting next to her at that performance. At the end of the first scene, she exclaimed: "Monterone, what a beautiful voice, but he is so thin!"

Many years later, a well known conductor, George Schick, later of the Metropolitan Opera, approached me to ask a personal favor. He had agreed to conduct a performance of *Rigoletto* at Carnegie Hall and was unhappy with the baritone who was singing Monterone. Would I oblige him by taking over on a moment's notice? He realized that at that time in my career I was past singing that role, but could I possibly do it under a different name, just for him? I agreed, and he put the name Giacomo Vittorio into the program for the role of Monterone. We had a good laugh when the New York Times review singled out this "Vittorio" in a supporting role for special favorable attention.

Pearl Harbor had come and gone. We were now at war, and it was only a question of time before I would become a member of the armed forces. In the meantime, we maintained a semblance of normality while the world around us was in flames. To continue functioning we needed to concentrate on day to day details of survival. Attention had to be focused on the immediate while we consciously evaded the grave emotional pressures that abounded.

Our little brownstone apartment was cheap and cozy, if only large enough for the two of us. Lack of money was a constant problem; while concentrating on singing I was also seeking any employment that might help pay for rent, food, and the other necessities of life. Marie's parents graciously took it upon them-selves to take care of our Andy, Marie's son from her previous marriage, then five years old, while we tried to weather these critical times. We, especially Marie, tried to spend as much time as possible with him, but much of his day to day care was left in the hands of a competent and loving nanny.

Yet, life was not quite as grim as these circumstances suggest. Recreation was inexpensive. We enjoyed marvelous Tom Collins drinks, sitting outside at "Topps" on 59th street, between Park and Madison Avenue, paying 25 cents for the drinks and snacks. Movies cost a quarter as well. I remember those anxiety-charged times with some warmth and fondness. Even my tours as a neighborhood air raid warden, sporting my white steel helmet, now seem almost romantic. Was it that we were young and felt omnipotent and invulnerable, or has the time that passed wiped out the anxiety and insecurity which must have been an integral part of our existence?

In the spring of 1942, I landed a summer engagement that proved to be one of the two most significant learning and maturing periods of my life as an artist. (The other was ten years later when Boris Goldowsky brought me to the Tanglewood Music Festival.) I was hired to participate in the Adirondack Arts Festival, located at a summer resort called "Green Mansions."

The producers were the conductor Isaac Van Grove and the stage director Felix Brentano. Again, pay was almost negligible, but Marie and I were given free room and board. I worked twelve to fifteen hours a day preparing opera performances, concerts and even major roles in dramatic productions under the guidance and direction of outstanding musicians and theater people. Felix Brentano had worked as an assistant to Max Reinhardt in Europe and Van Grove had a long and distinguished career in the U.S. Both accepted these assignments because they provided an opportunity to test productions which they planned to take to Broadway, a plan eventually executed.

Green Mansions, the resort where all this took place, was extraordinary. Nestled in the midst of the Adirondacks, on a beautiful lake near Warrensburg, New York, it catered to an elite group of intellectuals, teachers and academicians. Reputedly they were mainly attracted by the high caliber of the entertainment. Management took great pride in providing a varied choice of concerts, operas and shows, often starring nationally known talent, who appeared and worked with the resident company under the direction of the two producers.

In the summer of 1942, we performed in full concert recitals, often featuring contemporary composers whose works had to be freshly studied, memorized and performed in two or three days. We performed the Brentano production of Strauss' *Fledermaus* in an English version under the name of *Rosalinde* which opened that fall on Broadway with an almost identical cast. Virginia McWaters and I did an entire opera for two singers by Pergolesi (*La Serva Padrona*) in an elaborate fully costumed staging and prepared it in less than four days from the time we first saw the score. We staged a short opera, *There and Back* by Hindemith, participated in productions with such dancers as Mata and Hari, Arthur Mahoney and Thalia Mara, acted with Jack Gilford and performed plays by Gogol and others. The pianist accompanying the concerts and also performing solo was the later world famous Arthur Balsam. We even took the whole "Concert Show" for a paid appearance to Colgate University.

We lived and breathed music and theater from early morning to late at night, with short breaks for eating, swimming and tennis. Marie was with me, as was the collie- shepherd pup she gave me for our first wedding anniversary, Laurie, who was with us for the next seventeen years. Our accommodations were primitive but adequate; the meals which we shared with the guests were memorable.

My own, most significant experience of that summer was what I learned from Felix Brentano, the stage director. Felix had an enormous amount of magnetic dynamism, an excellent sense of humor, and was socially charming. Our intense work experience brought the whole cast and their families into close and intimate contact.

I was an inexperienced and somewhat stiff actor. I could follow directions, but I seemed to be going through the motions rather than conveying an integrated experience. Felix' directions were painfully detailed, and I found it difficult at rehearsals of *Serva*

Padrona to remember the newly memorized music, the text and all the gestures, movements and expressions that Felix demanded. One evening, without my knowledge, Felix asked Marie to stay away from rehearsals, two days before the scheduled first performance. That night, he scheduled a special night rehearsal for just him, the accompanist and myself. The more tired I became, and the harder I tried to carry out his directions, the more he criticized me, and kept putting me down. Finally, around three in the morning, I reached a point of exasperation when I was ready to cry with frustration, scream at him, attack him physically and walk out on the whole scene. He kept riding me, refusing to stop the rehearsal. And then something quite incredible took place. In the grip of total exhaustion, on the verge of breaking down, I felt something almost mystical happen to my body and mind. Suddenly, all the parts came together, and I was able to make the part of Uberto my own. Everything became natural and flowed easily. From that day on, I felt different when I stood on stage, able to coordinate my movements and to "fall into" the roles I was performing.

Perhaps only someone who has tried unsuccessfully to feel at home on a theater stage can appreciate how much this break-through meant to me. I understood later why Felix, experienced and stagewise, had planned deliberately to break down my resistance. It was painful, but worthwhile as a formative lesson for my future on stage.

Ten years later my experience at Green Mansions took on a new dimension. During the infamous McCarthy era, in my never ending search for supplemental income, I worked part time for the Voice of America, then under State Department auspices. My duties consisted of reading the morning news that was beamed to Vienna and Austria. In the company of some well known German-speaking actors like Werner Klemperer, Stephan Schnabel and others, reading from a prepared script, I proudly declared: "Hier spricht die Stimme Amerikas" (This is the voice of America.) Although my imagination does not reach into any way in which I could have compromised the security of my new homeland, short of sending coded messages by my voice pitch, I had to undergo a security clearance.

For about six months I heard from neighbors and friends, including some who were abroad at that time, that FBI personnel had interviewed them with regard to my consideration for a "government position." Finally, I was invited to present myself for an interview (interrogation?) at a federal building in New York. As I felt quite secure in the knowledge that I had nothing to hide, I looked forward to the occasion without any conscious anxiety; in fact, I anticipated a pleasant, challenging exchange.

As I arrived in a typical small government office, two men representing almost stereotypical FBI types (tall, slim, neatly dressed and groomed) introduced themselves and asked me to sit. They informed me that I was free to refuse answers to any questions, but, if I were interested in working for the Voice of America, I was compelled to answer truthfully. That was fine with me, and for about two hours they fired away, mostly questions that I could answer easily. Some of the queries were based on erroneous background information which I tried to clarify, not knowing whether I was successful or not. For instance, they confused the Screen Actors Guild of which I was a member (anybody appearing in an American film had to be) with the Screen Directors Guild which apparently was considered a Communist Front. They implied that a fascist Austrian pre-war organization, the "Heimwehr," represented the democratic factions in Austria (in fact, less than five percent voted for them), etc. One interesting question stood out. They asked would I picket a place that would refuse to serve blacks, and I answered I would not, because temperamentally I was not the picketing type. They then asked whether I had ever slept with a black woman (I believe the term then was "colored"), and I responded that I had not because I had not had the opportunity. And so it went for about two hours.

They thanked me for my cooperation; I believe we shook hands, and on my way out the door, quite suddenly, we were in the middle of a Hollywood scenario. "Oh, incidentally, where were you in the summer of 1942?" Somewhat taken aback, I began to figure backwards, and finally answered: "At the Arts Festival at Green Mansions."

"Aha!" I sat down again and asked: "What is that about?" "We ask the questions here." Somewhat puzzled I wondered what caused that change of tone? "How do you explain your presence there?" I tried to express my bewilderment, proceeded to describe the type of important hard work we had been doing there, and mentioned some of the celebrities that had been there with me. "You mean to tell us that you never saw the *Daily Worker* lying around, and did not notice any clandestine meetings?" I could assure them with all the conviction I was capable of that the only thing I ever saw lying around there were music scores and scripts of plays. They responded with a neutral, therapeutic "Hmm." Finally, they told me that the owners of Green Mansions were among the most generous contributors to the Communist Party of America, and that the place was known as a hot bed of subversion. I do not know whether that was true, or, for that matter, whether they believed me. Shortly afterwards, I was no longer being called in by the Voice of America.

In the fall of 1942, a new engagement loomed. A highly respectable new opera company, called with great originality "The New Opera Company," had been founded under the administrative leadership of a former Hungarian pianist, Mme. Mero-Irion. Among its conductors were internationally known musicians like Fritz Stiedry, Fritz Busch and Emil Cooper. Among the stage directors were Felix Brentano and Hans Busch; Van Grove, too, was on the musical staff. Their schedule included new productions of Verdi's *Macbeth*, Offenbach's *La Vie Parisienne*, Moussorgsky's *Fair of Sorotchinsk*, and a new work by the American composer Walter Damrosch. All performances were in English. The company took pride in presenting what they considered top young "American" singers. Not only did their planning offer marvelous opportunities for artists who had not yet reached anywhere close to stardom to work under high quality leadership, but it also enabled the company to meet the humongous budget costs involved in presenting opera. We performed the operas at the Broadway Theater, while a season of classical operettas (*Rosalinde* and *The Merry Widow*) was performed at the 44th Street Theater.

I was engaged to sing some small to medium parts with the company, including one in the world premiere of Damrosch's *Opera Cloak*. This gave me an opportunity to work with a reputable, highly professional opera outfit, and led to my first favorable mention by New York music critics.

Damrosch, a much respected and then quite elderly musician, was to conduct his own work. All musical preparations were done by assistant conductors under his occasional supervision, as his health was apparently not quite up to the strains of rehearsals. When it was time for the first orchestra dress rehearsal under the baton of the maestro himself, something quite dramatic happened. Damrosch began to conduct by raising his arm, then lowered it for a downbeat. Unfortunately, he was not strong enough to maintain the tempo for the rest of the bar, so that the music became slower and slower within each bar and then within each phrase. I remember how everybody gasped in shock at the rehearsal, as we tried to use our reserves of breath to keep up with the ever slowing tempi. Significantly, I cannot recall what happened at the actual premiere. I suspect that one of the assistants who had prepared the work took over, but I am no longer sure of it. The reviews were gentle with the composer, and kind to the singers.

Mme. Irion, the general manager, was quite a character. She had a very thick Hungarian accent and a good sense of humor. During one dress rehearsal, when I was wearing an officer's white tights, it was *Pique Dame* I believe, she sent up the stage manager to suggest that I wear a jockstrap. I, who had grown up with boxer shorts, learned of another American institution.

In the production of *The Merry Widow* at the other house, Jan Kiepura and Martha Eggert, both with heavy accents and a fine reputation in European films, affectionately known as "Ham and Eggs," sang the leads. The stage manager, Paul Feigay, approached

Mme. Irion discreetly during one of the rehearsals and whispered to her: "Mme. Irion, Miss Eggert is singing 'Vilia, oh Vilia you vitch of the voods'!" Whereupon Mme. Irion was reputed to have answered: "So vat!"

Some time later, as a soldier on leave, I visited New York, and went to show off my uniform to Mme. Irion. We chatted for a while, and I mentioned that my office at Camp Ritchie, the War Department Intelligence Training Center, was in the same building in which Lt. Ernest McChesney, a former tenor with the company, was housed. Mme. Irion threw up her hands, and exclaimed in mock exasperation: "Oh my God, two singers in Intelligence! How are ve going to vin the var?!"

And so the season passed. I was another valuable experience richer and could point to some polite press notices. The struggle for survival resumed in full force, while the local draft board was breathing down my neck more and more closely. The final induction notice came in April of 1943.

Meanwhile, another Broadway musical showed some interest in me. In the midst of all the world's turmoil, I was about to add an engagement in the famous Ziegfeld Follies to my resume. The *Ziegfeld Follies of 1943* starred Milton Berle, Ilona Massey, Arthur Treacher, a bevy of "longstemmed American beauties" as showgirls, a fine corps de ballet, lots of acts, comedians, straight men and Manfred Hecht as a "Saroyan character." I also managed a male quartet of singers, billed as "The Vikings," and sang solos like: "I Want What I Want, When I Want It." The wardrobe was splendid, and the Vikings' costumes outshone, I am sure, the uniforms President Nixon chose in later years for the White House Guards. I still recall one of my lines as The Saroyan Character: "The Ziegfeld Follies, (pause), Lust, Greed, Desire, Money, Passion, Nudity. (pause) It's wonderful!"

The rehearsals were fun. It was hard work, but, nobody, including me, took it seriously. We had a fine director, John Murray Anderson, who had a delightful sense of humor that softened his anger at even the most outrageous situations. He addressed every cast member with names he invented for them. Milton Berle (for good reason) was called "Stalin." I was "Metropolitan," the showgirls were "The Bruisers," and so on.

We finally opened in Boston at the Schubert Theater, and I went through the familiar rehearsal and out of town opening experience. What was new were the large number of cast parties, promoted by the Schubert Organization. There were invitations to various nightclubs where Milton Berle mixed it up as guest with the working comedians. The various backers of the show outdid each other with entertaining the cast, and introducing us to their friends. Yet, Boston and its theatrical district still felt cold and alien to me.

I remember the backstage notice, signed by Mayor Curley, who had just been released from jail because of a corruption conviction, informing us that no swearing or use of dirty language would be tolerated backstage. Violators would be punished to the full measure of the law.

Boston offered Durgin Parks Restaurant, which prided itself on serving the finest and largest steaks in the midst of wartime rationing. The city was also famous for its burlesque show at the "Old Howard." Marie, who had joined me in Boston, and about eight of the very tall and statuesque showgirls, decided that we would all go to the Old Howard to see the show. I was to act as the "chaperon." We were admitted as guests of the management. As we entered the theater and walked to our seats, nine stunning women and I, the heads of all the men in the audience turned towards us, and for quite a while attention was fixed on my companions rather than on the stage. The show was moderately amusing, especially due to the incredible acrobatics of some of the strippers.

We all decided to pay a courtesy call backstage. For unknown reasons, we had to pass through a vegetable store to reach the stage entrance. I can still smell the onions, radishes, lettuce and other legumes that surrounded us before we entered the perfumed dressing rooms of our colleagues who worked in the burlesque house.

Time out of uniform was shrinking rapidly. When the show moved to the Forrest Theater in Philadelphia before opening at the Wintergarden in New York, the entire atmosphere seemed to change radically. In contrast to the snow in Boston, Philadelphia seemed clean and smelled of the approaching spring. The builders of the Forrest Theater had apparently forgotten to include dressing rooms in their planning, so that all performers had to reach the stage from the dressing rooms either by a somewhat difficult basement passage, or by crossing a back alley out in the open. Whenever the weather permitted, that was the way we chose. Some neighboring factories perfumed the air around the theater district with delicious whiffs of tobacco and coffee.

After the show, we occasionally went to see a movie in the all night movie houses, took walks and enjoyed spring and being alive. Perhaps the risk of impending military service in war time made life seem especially precious and eminently worth living.

We opened in New York to some critical success, and two weeks later I reported for induction into the U.S. Army. Those were hectic weeks. There were some small cast parties for my farewell, a few gifts, and I was gone.

Emotionally, like everyone else facing military service, I was confused, conflicted, scared, and hating to leave Marie and the little comforts we had grown accustomed to together. Perhaps these feelings were enhanced by the painful memories of earlier separations. Once more in my life I was facing what was unknown, uncertain, and frightening. The one thing I was certain of was that life would never be the same, and that another part of my passage had ended. I also knew that whatever would come was inevitable and I had no choice but to accept it, and make the best of it.

VII — "THIS IS THE ARMY, MR. HECHT..."

Early on a dreary, rainy April morning I reported for "induction" into the armed forces, about to share the experience of millions who had come before me and of millions who would follow. The group of scared-looking young men who, just as I, had been through all the preliminary medical screenings were now more or less ready to go to war.

I not only looked scared, I was scared. Also confused and bewildered. Yet challenged and excited. Above all, I was cold. Cold, because it was chilly outside, and cold because I was frightened.

Names were called, and we were divided into small groups, supposed to stay together under the "command" of an acting corporal, appointed spontaneously from among us. I was chosen for that job. Instantly, my spirits lifted, and I felt that this was a promising omen for a brilliant army career.

Together with a large group of soldiers to be, the men "under my command" proceeded to the train that brought us to the reception center at Camp Upton on Long Island. We arrived as a motley crew, still scared but now also quite tired, and began the orientation and induction process. Somewhere along the line we were welcomed, sworn in and fed.

What followed seemed endless periods of standing around, waiting, and being yelled at. We marched (from now on we were no longer walking, just marching) from one place to another, filled out forms, were lectured, and eventually were issued clothes and equipment.

In the environment of the camp, civilian clothes felt uncomfortable and inappropriate. There was something ill fitting and awkward about civilian shoes on the dusty soil of parade grounds. I was relieved when I was issued my army boots and the rest of the "stuff" that represented all I would need in the way of clothes, toilet articles, eating utensils, tents, backpacks and canteens. Loaded down with two full barracks bags, I staggered to the barracks and the bed I was assigned to.

On the way to our new accommodations, men in fatigue uniforms, apparently those who had been inducted a day or two earlier and who now considered themselves experienced veterans shouted at us: "watch the hook!" I soon found out that this was the standard treatment that all newcomers received; it was supposed to amuse the "old-timers," and frighten the recruits about the impending series of shots and vaccinations. I already was so anxious that the prospect of inoculations no longer made any difference.

In the midst of all the activities, I began to understand the rationale for the atmosphere and routine of the reception center. The army let you know quite a few things that did not need to be spelled out. Obviously, from now on you were at the mercy of the Service as represented by your superiors. They were in a position either to take care of you and make you feel good, or to make life quite miserable for you, if you did not comply. It was their prerogative to assign you to relatively pleasant or highly unpleasant tasks, light or very strenuous duties. You could be rendered totally fatigued, achy to the breaking point and depressed; or, you could become "one of the boys," find support from your comrades and prove that you could take it as well as, or better than, the next man. It was up to you. You could try to buck the system and risk having it break you; you could join it with more or less enthusiasm and take pride in becoming "the best soldier you can be"; or, you could try to learn how to survive within the system and still manage situations in such a way that you retained some personal pride as well as some freedom of choice and action.

On that first afternoon I felt the potential for all three of these alternatives in various permutations. I even began to feel twinges of resentment at being pushed around in what seemed a rather aimless fashion; but, I also knew that I was finally about to become active in a war that mattered to me enormously, even beyond mere duty to my new country; yet, the old necessary ways of surviving coercion and authoritarian manipulation began to emerge.

That first evening we were run through a batch of tests while trying to keep awake. Never before had I taken tests under time pressure; it seemed baffling to me to have to skip questions rather than to take time to think of the right answer. I found out much later that I did pretty well on the tests measuring general intelligence. However, tests of my mechanical knowledge were a different story. All I could do was to stare at words describing tools or machinery; I did not know what they meant, I did not even have an inkling of what they might mean.

Finally, we were permitted to fall on our cots and close our eyes. But this release was not meant to last. At two thirty a.m. we were awakened to report for K.P. The Service was clearly eager to impress the recruits with the powers at its disposal. As we staggered to the mess hall to perform our scrubbing and cleaning duties, the old survival techniques began to take over. Blind obedience to authority had always been a problem for me. I hated what I was doing and my mind became busy trying to think of how to escape from what felt like harassment.

Similar experiences from my past taught me my first lesson of how to survive in the army by looking out for myself. I discovered that a few soldiers managed to be assigned to special duty, which meant that they were issued a pass which allowed them the run of the camp while they were engaged in whatever these "special assignments" required of them. They could no longer be stopped by any passing noncom and drafted for some menial labor; also, they were exempt from the drudgery of the barracks routine. As these special assignment soldiers tended to stay in camp somewhat longer than the three or so days it usually took to transfer recruits to a basic training unit anywhere in the United States, they were often quartered in small private rooms in the barracks. To acquire such a pass became my objective. At the first opportunity, I found the post chapel where the three chaplains of the major faiths had their offices. I was eager to let the Jewish Chaplain know of my extensive experience in performing the musical part of religious services in various temples, including Temple Emanu-el in New York. I also hinted that, in the light of my past engagements, I could be quite useful to the religious services of the other denominations. Captain Sherman informed me that he had an assistant, and therefore had no opening, even for as desirable a helper as I might be. But, he arranged to hear me sing for him in the chapel, accompanied by the organist who was assistant to the Protestant chaplain.

I gave my all to some oratorio and "sacred solos," and was rewarded, when the Catholic chaplain, a wonderfully humorous and gentle priest, Captain McGrath, found that he had an opening for an assistant. I could hardly contain my joy, when, armed with a special duty pass, I ran all the way back to my company area, and reported the news to my Sergeant. Instantly, I became a member of the privileged elite.

The absurd humor of my situation did not escape me. I, a Jewish refugee from Hitler's persecution, now a member of an army at war with Hitler, had just won a brief respite from the drudgery of the reception center by becoming the assistant to the Catholic chaplain. I felt wonderful, and I felt no guilt. "Only in America..."

My duties consisted of being of general assistance to my boss, Father McGrath, and included my vocal participation in all religious services, Catholic, Jewish and Protestant. The organist and I soon became friends, and we enjoyed making music together. In addition to the Jewish services on Friday and Saturday, we participated on an average Sunday in up to nine religious services. Morning services, Catholic and Protestant, hospital services, including a special service on the isolated venereal ward, services at the prison, vesper services in the late afternoon and a Christian Science service. Trevor and I played and sang them all, and felt that we were earning our privates' pay.

Once, at the Venereal Ward, he chose the hymn: "Clap your hands all ye people;" it took me a while to "get it." The hardest part was listening to nine sermons in one day. But we managed to survive them and at the end of the day made our way to the PX, where we partook liberally of army beer.

The days at Camp Upton stretched to about four months which

gave me a wonderful opportunity to acclimatize to the army. I learned how to survive in the system; never again did I feel the pain of being out of control that had plagued me on the first two days. I gained some confidence, perhaps too much, that I could play some part in what was happening or was about to happen to me. Not a large part, but just enough so I would not have to suffer from, what was to me, an excruciating feeling of powerlessness. I met many other soldiers, made new friends, enjoyed their company, and learned from those who were more experienced or wiser.

Camp Upton, one of two army reception centers for the New York metropolitan area, also received its share of entertainers. Special Services put on shows for the soldiers and I was invited to participate, which I did with great pleasure. In the course of rehearsals I came to know a number of men who, as civilians, had been on stage. I especially cherish the memory of my friendship with the late wonderful dancer José Limon, a great artist and a gracious human being. In our first performance together, he danced while I sang Cole Porter's "Begin the Beguine" on an outdoor stage. The many evenings we spent talking together about our lives and aspirations considerably lightened the burden of those early days.

Camp Upton also offered a chance to maintain easy telephone contact with Marie; Father McGrath did not object to my using his phone in the chapel when he did not need it, and I took ample advantage of this opportunity. When the telephone rang, and it was Marie, he would ask her when she would cook a decent steak for him and begged her to tell me to get my butt out of his office and to stop using his phone. Then he would turn and yell at me to get my feet off his desk as he smiled and handed me the phone.

But, the most wonderful and joyful event was my first overnight pass to New York. Patchogue, the railroad station serving the camp, was only hours away from the city; on that first occasion I felt excited and exhilarated when I saw Marie standing at the Long Island Railroad Station in the Manhattan terminal. In my well pressed dress uniform, I was a proud member of the Armed Forces. No longer was I concerned about being stared at by wives and relatives of other servicemen. Whether they, in fact, thought it or not, I felt that they had been wondering: "What is wrong with this guy, why is he not in uniform?" Well, now I was, and that part of it felt great.

Walking through New York on a balmy spring evening, with Marie on my arm, after a drink and a decent meal at a good restaurant, on our way to a more intimate reunion in the privacy of our apartment, I could not complain too much about life as a soldier in war time. What a thrill it was to sleep with my wife on a real bed, behind locked doors: no snoring sounds, no commands, no whistles.

The pleasures I just described were experienced on the most superficial level of my consciousness. Not very far beneath, there lurked a keen inkling that the serious events taking place around me would soon affect my personal life very deeply; possibly, very tragically. I had flashes of awareness, but I also knew that there was no point in my dwelling on the possibility of future dramatic happenings. What limited control I had was restricted to one-day-at-a-time activities. Without full consciousness, I was applying a large measure of denial to the menacing forces outside and within me, and so I was able to function without undue anxiety.

In one of the many sermons that I was exposed to, the preacher looked seriously at the congregation of freshly recruited soldiers. He invited them to look at those sitting around them and reminded them that, at the end of the war, one in three could be expected to be dead or seriously injured. A cold shiver went down my spine and exposed the raw nerve that I had been trying to ignore.

In addition to those elemental fears, I was, for the second time in my life, experiencing feelings of loss and separation from the home and family that I had become attached to. The fate of my parents was totally unknown and continued to weigh heavily on me. I had no means of communicating with them and the Nazis were still winning the war; the myth of the invincible German War Machine had not been destroyed yet.

But, here I was, reasonably comfortable, getting accustomed to the uniform; the army helped repair my varicose veins surgically, so that I could go on to further training requiring standing and moving for extended periods. Some of the soldiers I hung around with mentioned that they were being asked questions about me by army investigators; this meant to me that the processing of my application for American citizenship was proceeding and my departure from Camp Upton would not be long in coming.

Several men I met briefly at Upton went to some lengths to find me in the sixties and seventies. They wanted me to meet their families, and shared with me how deeply they had been affected when, during their first tumultuous army days, they had accidentally walked by the chapel and heard me rehearsing classical music. I was very moved by their response and felt privileged for having been able to provide some meaningful comfort to them.

My days at Camp Upton were coming to an end. Army red tape notwithstanding, some clerical process was put in motion that decided it was time to get Hecht into the real army. And so it was. With a large group of other men, I received orders to report to Camp Grant, Illinois, for basic training.

In the best army tradition, my destination was classified but leaked almost as soon as I was told to prepare for shipping out. My friend José managed to convey to Marie by phone that I would be within about a hundred miles of Chicago. She did some spectacular detective work and, within three days of my arrival at Camp Grant, I received a telegram notifying me of her address in Rockford, Illinois, the town next to the Camp. With the help of the Jewish Welfare Board which ran the local USO (United Service Organization), she had obtained a furnished room and the promise of a job on arrival; and there she was, accompanied by our dog, Laurie.

What a privilege it was to embrace her when I had my first pass, what joy to have a temporary home away from the camp. It became even more of a treat when I eventually was permitted to spend my free nights and days off the post in our own rooms.

A pass now meant not only a night on the town in Rockford as it did for most others, but a chance to be with my wife. My eagerness to get on the bus to town was great, as was my anxiety, frustration and helplessness, when, for many, often arbitrary reasons, I could not get a pass. Yet, I knew that I was very lucky and privileged to have the chance of a family life during basic army training.

Camp Grant was a training center for the Medical Department, and I suppose I was sent there because I had been to medical school; once processed, I was assigned to a training battalion which was to prepare me to become a litter bearer, first aid man, or to be sent for hospital duty. As assignments went, it made some sense and I certainly preferred it to the notorious infantry training centers in the deep South.

There were aspects of the training that I enjoyed. I did not mind the new experience of living in a large tent together with five other men, all from the Northeast and fairly compatible. In warm weather the flaps could be rolled up, and the gentle breezes of the Illinois plains cooled the tent. The fellows were nice, some interesting, and we developed a sort of camaraderie which permitted us to become closer.

I liked the drilling in the fresh air, and, to my amazement, did not even mind some of the marching; this did not extend to forced marches or those infamous twenty mile hikes with full field pack. By and large, the officers and noncoms were a decent lot doing their job.

One of the platoon leaders, a lieutenant from an Italian-American family in New York, had a collection of classical records and, learning of my interest, invited me to listen with him. On an off-duty afternoon when I could not get a pass, we listened in his tent to a marvelous recording of *La Boheme* and the grim aspects of the current reality receded into nothing while we escaped to the world of Mimi and Rudolfo and Puccini.

The cultural climate prevailing during basic training was like a desert. I felt desperately thirsty for classical music and was delighted to find an occasional oasis. There were also some musical activities in Rockford which welcomed servicemen, and the local USO did have classical records. One of the most frequently heard complaints from friends who ended up in the Southern camps was that they could not escape the blaring din of hillbilly music wherever they turned.

During these first few months I was always exhausted. When I was not physically active, especially during class lectures, it took an enormous effort to keep my eyes open. Early wake-up calls allowed for very little sleep, especially in view of the strenuous physical schedule; also, in retrospect, I can see that I was mildly depressed. In spite of all the physical exercise, I gained thirty pounds during that period. Army food in those early days was vile. We had apprentice cooks who used an enormous amount of fat, and, until food trays with compartments arrived, we had all the food put on one dish. Considering that stew and ice cream often blended on one plate, there must have been some powerful reason why I was eating enough to gain all this weight.

From my earliest memories on, I felt that intake of food was pleasurable and reassuring. It seemed that a full stomach gave me a sense of strength and well being, or, as I learned later, reduced my anxiety. The months of basic training provided an ample supply of that. Although I have no specific recollection of having to change uniform sizes, I am sure that I must have given the supply sergeant his share of problems.

As autumn gave way to colder weather, the delights of outdoor living diminished rapidly. Although the tents were heated, the camping-out trips and nights under pup-tents were bone-chilling. I am willing to concede that guard duty in polar areas may have been even colder, but with parkas, boots and all, guard duty on a December night in Illinois must be hard to beat for sheer icy physical discomfort.

Yet, there were some charms to the newly found experience of winter in Middle America, in the smallest city I had ever lived in. The hospitality of the civilian population was truly overwhelming. There was no sense of discrimination, not because of my accent, nor my Jewishness, not even because of my low military rank. Marie and I were welcomed with open arms, invited to splendid dinners and outings at every possible occasion, and were able to participate in several musical events. There was something special about the ice cold air, the frosty windows of the lovely snow-covered houses, the warm reception our hosts extended to us, the crackling logs in the fireplace, the delicious wafts of dinner cooking. I could understand where all the sentimental postcards depicting Thanksgiving and Christmas had found their true origin.

As word spread that I possessed a trained singing voice (I did nothing to squelch the rumors), I was invited to participate in and help organize a battalion show. That I did, and, as the Commanding Officer of Camp Grant attended the performance and enjoyed it, I was asked whether I would mind singing in some war bond shows that Camp Grant sent out to communities within a radius of sixty or so miles. These events, organized by Special Services, were intended to promote sales of war bonds; it was understood that my taking part in them would be in addition to my other duties, but that I could expect some relief on the day of the show.

I jumped at the opportunity with the result that a "hold" was placed on my name once basic training was over. That meant that instead of being shipped to the Pacific theater of war, as most of my fellow trainees were, I was attached, "unassigned," to a head-quarters unit and given a variety of light duties. I recall with some discomfort my delight at being spared, at least temporarily, the arduous combat duty of carrying litters with the front units in the Pacific isles. The survivor in me reveled at this fortunate turn of events, and conquered some guilt feelings and any misbegotten eagerness to display my bravery.

During the day, I went to "Clerks' School" to be trained for the duties of a company clerk, and to study typing and other clerical skills. On some afternoons and evenings, with other entertainers and the band, I mounted a truck or a bus, and traveled around Rockford, DeKalb and Aurora, all in Illinois, and a few places in Wisconsin as well. It was an exciting way to see some of the country.

Once we got there, we had a quick rehearsal, either on a local bandstand or in a hall, and then put on a show in the evening, come rain, shine, or snow. I was singing some semiclassical and standard numbers; with us was an excellent comedian-magician, whose name, Francis X. Finnegan, still sticks in my mind. Also with us was a handsome Irish tenor, and, I believe, a dancer. We must have put on a rather decent show, judging not only from the reaction of our audiences, but from the fact that I enjoyed watching and hearing the others in the show again and again.

I now lived in well built barracks when I was not free to go home for the night, and life was more than bearable. Of course, we knew that all that bliss could not last for very long. After I made some inquiries, I was offered the opportunity to apply for training in Army Intelligence. I felt strongly that, once my time had come to go overseas, I would much prefer to be in the European Theater of War, and that my knowledge of languages and my European background could offer a contribution. So I applied, and, by now understanding the ways of the army, promptly forgot about it.

Earlier in my basic training, Marie and I ran into a chain of problems that centered on our shepherd-collie, Laurie, and her presence in our apartment. Retrospectively, the worries and vicissitudes about our beloved dog seem of small weight. But impotent as we were in affecting the major crises of our lives, our problems about Laurie caused a disproportionate amount of excitement, pain and concern.

The landlady who owned the inexpensive quarters we could barely afford served notice that she would not permit us *and* our dog to stay. It was Laurie or us.

Marie, faced with this quandary, called me at camp. Her agitation was quickly shared by me. Emergency conferences (through channels) with the first sergeant and the company commander brought help. With the provision that she would not interfere with training activities, Laurie could become our company mascot. Hallelujah! The whole affair became a company event; Laurie was welcomed, given "dog tags" that carried the inscription "WAAC" (Women's Auxiliary Army Corps) "Auxiliary Laurie," a serial number and the identity of our training company, platoon and squad.

So far so good. Laurie loved it, I loved it, and the guys loved her. She nestled on my cot, occasionally accompanied us on marches if they were not too strenuous, and, with the exception of some minor grumbling by the fellows when we scrubbed and cleaned our quarters for inspection, everything worked smoothly, until that old "devil" sex created a major crisis. Laurie, who had not been spayed, came into heat. Hordes of more or less elegant suitors began to show up around our tent, serenading, wooing, and frequently leaving their calling cards against the tent flaps! Another problem of serious proportions was at hand.

I could not even conceive of an argument that could help avoid summary banishment; but, I was able to get a few hours off to try and organize some emergency rescue. The courting cavaliers, now including the captain's Irish setter, continued to cavort around my tent, while Marie and I took off. With the help of some Rockford friends, we tried to find a farmer who would grant Laurie temporary asylum. We did find a fine gentleman, six miles from camp, willing to extend the hospitality of his barn. Another crisis conquered! Much relieved, yet with heavy hearts, we entrusted WAAC Auxiliary Laurie to the farmer's care, with his permission to check periodically on her welfare.

This should have taken care of the problem, but Laurie did not choose to cooperate. A few days after her move, when I called the farmer to check on her well-being, he told me that Laurie had torn her chain and had taken off. Marie and I were both heartbroken and began efforts to find her. We advertised in the local paper, which quickly recognized a good dog story. Articles full of biographical details about her and us began to appear under the heading: "WAAC Auxiliary Laurie AWOL!" and readers were advised daily of the search for the missing company recruit.

A few days later, returning from training, I found Laurie lying on my cot. She was exhausted, panting, a torn rope around her neck, but wagging her tail at me. As I was hugging her, my heart was racing and I vowed to myself never again to abandon her if that was humanly possible. I really could not believe my eyes; I still find it incredible that she was able to find the camp, and, among the thousands of tents, my area and my cot.

A quick decision was made that we would find another apartment in town. Under no circumstances were we going to leave her again. Aided by a lot of good will from all our sources, including the Rockford newspaper, we succeeded in soon finding quarters for all of us.

Ah, but that was not the end of the trials and tribulations surrounding the tale of our shepherd-collie. Alas, the captain's Irish setter had scored, and Laurie was clearly with child. On a cold winter night, she emitted a little yelp while lying on our bed, and she delivered the first of eight little soft furry balls that turned out to be puppies. We outfitted a carton with newspapers, watched Laurie lick her puppies clean, made them all comfortable, and waited for the ax to fall. We did not have to wait long. The next morning I was called to the telephone in the orderly tent to hear my wife's tremulous voice. The landlady had informed her that she and her nine dogs better "get the hell out of there in a hurry." However, Marie reassured me, not to worry, she was going to take care of things.

And, in fact, she did. After calling several service organizations and announcing to them that she was a serviceman's wife, in trouble and in need of help, she hit on the local Shriners' group. Whoever answered the phone and heard her introduction was so relieved that she was clearly not seeking an abortionist or threatening suicide, that he offered a cozy spot in their boiler room, where the new mother and her eight offspring could rest comfortably. An unlocked entrance permitted us access so that we could feed and clean the brood.

Again, Lady Luck had been good to us. Laurie and her pups were well protected and warm, we found yet another, more desirable place to live, and eventually, the puppies, all of them with setter characteristics, were adopted, and Laurie was again permitted to share our home. We knew better than to mention matters of paternity to my commanding officer. I conjure up easily, with a smile, the scene of Laurie and her eight puppies cuddling around the boiler, while five or six Shriners in full regalia were playing with them.

Mother, 1917

Father, 1917
Front row, left

Mother, on Vacation in the
Dolomites

Parents and I in the
Dolomites, 1927

Vienna, Lichtensteinstrasse 25
The House I Grew Up In

1952, NBC–TV, Rosenkavalier
First on Right: Hecht as Faninal

CBS–TV Live, 1951
Traviata
Right: Hecht. Center: Lawrence Tibbett &
Elaine Malbin

112

Laurie, I, and Marie,
1952

Marie & I, 1996

VIII — "MY COUNTRY 'TIS OF THEE...

While stationed at Camp Grant, I became a United States citizen. I was no longer an alien, an expatriate Austrian, a man who was a Jew without a country. Symbolically, at least, I was a full-fledged American, entitled to an American passport and to all the privileges that United States citizenship conferred. I felt deep, unquestioned loyalty to my new country, and pride at being officially part of its citizenry.

The ceremony at the court house in Rockford was by itself not especially impressive. There were so many feelings and thoughts buzzing through me, that all I could sense clearly was that time was needed to sort them all out. I have read about and watched on TV many such ceremonies and I have spoken to many foreign-born people who have acquired their U.S. citizenship papers. I cannot quite identify with the tearful "kissing the hallowed ground" reaction. This sort of display is just not part of my emotional repertoire. Nor can I understand those who had sought American citizenship as a matter of convenience, and who kept on referring to their country of birth in idealized terms while being highly critical of most things in America.

Perhaps one must have lived without the protection of a sovereign country and have experienced a constant threat to life and limb to appreciate fully what it means to be an American citizen. Perhaps one must have been through the glory of finding a safe and hospitable haven; perhaps also, one must have been able to dispose of the rose-colored glasses of nostalgia that tend to glamorize memories of the past. Only then may one be able to recognize emotionally the weaknesses and defects in the country of one's birth; and, in turn, only then can a person be ready to fully value and love the unique features of American life, society, political system and philosophy. At that juncture of my life, I was filled with patriotic fervor as I awaited the further twists and turns of my army career.

This was not the first time that I had applied for citizenship. The law required a waiting period of much less than the usual five years of U.S. residence for a legal immigrant married to an American citizen. In 1942, long before I had joined the Armed Forces, Marie and I, accompanied by her father, Harry, had appeared for an appointment in front of a U.S. immigration officer in New York. My father-in-law, born in New York, was a rather elegant, kindly, quiet gentleman with a sense of humor. He tended to dress in a conservative, business-executive fashion, and favored bowler hats.

We all faced a stern looking official who spent some time shuffling the documents before him. They included my green card, Marie's birth certificate, her divorce papers, and our marriage certificate. He looked at us accusingly.

He: "What do you want from me?"

I: "On the basis of my marriage to an American citizen I would like to apply for accelerated second papers."

He: "What makes you think you are married to this lady?"

I: "You are looking at our marriage certificate."

He: "This is just a piece of paper."

I: "Well, I know, but does it not certify that we are married?"

He: "It might show that this lady is a bigamist; it does not show that she is legally married to you." At this point I realized that my father-in-law's complexion which was usually quite light, had turned to a waxen pallor.

I: "Would you mind helping me understand just what you mean?"

He: "Sure. See, all these so called documents about her divorce in Mexico? She was not a resident there, neither was her former husband. They ain't worth the paper they're written on. We don't recognize Mexican divorces. Whatever may have happened between you and her and that Justice of the Peace, certainly in the eyes of the Federal Government, has no validity whatsoever. You've got to be divorced before you can get married again in these here United States. Capish? You, young lady, better get yourself a valid divorce before you try any marriages, or you can be charged with bigamy."

I "capished" all right. Notwithstanding the fact that Marie's former husband, a lawyer, currently working as a district attorney had remarried; never mind the certifications and court orders from Juarez; in the eyes of the Federal Government we were not married. We looked at each other, and to Harry's embarrassment said together: "Isn't it more fun to live in sin?" Harry, to his credit, did not bat an eye. "I wonder what comes next," he said "Let's go and have a drink!" And so we did.

My naturalization now had to wait until I had satisfied the waiting requirements for a member of the Armed Forces. Nobody had promised that it was going to be easy.

After the excitement about Laurie and my induction as a U.S. citizen, events started moving with surprising rapidity.

My appendix started to act up and I underwent surgery. In those days that meant that, for the next six months, I would be placed on limited duty status. After my discharge from the hospital, I was assigned as clerk to one of the training units. It seemed that, for a while at least, we could settle down, and that the time was ripe to apply for a furlough and to bring Andy to live with us in Rockford. We had a delightful reunion in New York, and returned, all prepared, we thought, for a few months of normality. I reported immediately to my company, and, was informed that — congratulations — my application for transfer to Military Intelligence had been approved by the War Department and I was on confidential orders to be shipped out the next morning. Destination: very hush, hush, War Department Military Intelligence Training Center, Camp Ritchie, Maryland. Although I was pleased and excited by this change, this also meant an immediate trip back East and a complete shift of all plans for the family. I felt overwhelmed, but fatalistically optimistic that somehow things would turn out all right. Anyway, I could do nothing to change what was. There was just barely time to inform Marie, and off I went. Camp Ritchie was so highly confidential that the information clerk at the Baltimore Railroad Station where I had to change trains, noting my accent when I asked about track locations, interrupted after my first "excuse me" with "The train to Ritchie will be on track four."

In many ways it was an extraordinary camp, but security did not even extend to the beautiful books of matches that the post exchange proudly issued. They all bore the emblems of the various branches of intelligence for which the camp was preparing its trainees, and carried the inscription M.I.T.C.-Military Intelligence Training Center. To my knowledge Ritchie was the only training center that operated on an eight-day week. Every eighth day was a day off, called "Ban-Day," after the Commanding Officer's name, "Banfield."

I discovered that I had been shipped there by mistake. My classification for limited duty due to recent abdominal surgery disqualified me for the somewhat strenuous intelligence training. Yet, War Department orders superseded any Camp Grant orders to return me for duty there. Marie tried hard, even with the cooperation of Camp Grant's C.O., to correct the error, without success.

I was temporarily assigned to a holding company in Ritchie. One day, I was sent on an errand to the personnel office, where I discovered, to our mutual surprise, that the personnel officer was a woman captain, formerly a fine soprano with whom I had participated in various workshops of the National Orchestra Association. We greeted each other enthusiastically, and sat down for a chat about my military future. It was clear that I could not get back to Grant, but, if I wanted to stay in Ritchie, she could get me an assignment.

And so it went. I was sent for an interview with a wonderful guy, Col. Dooley, then the head of the intelligence office at the camp. As a civilian he had worked with the Juvenile Division of the New York Police Department. He was a distinguished looking, tall, slender, gray-haired man with a slight Irish brogue, marvelously fair at all times, with a good sense of humor and a thorough knowledge of army politics. He interviewed me at some length before we both realized that he had the wrong file in front of him; there apparently was another Hecht in Camp Ritchie. By that time he discovered that he liked me enough to want me to work for him. Thus, I became the first foreign-born soldier to work in the post intelligence office of the Intelligence Training Center, where most of the work dealt with the investigation of foreign-born personnel being trained for sensitive assignments after completion of training.

My duties were mostly clerical; but, as the others assigned to the office as investigators, all lawyers, were also enlisted men rather than officers, there was a pleasant collegiate atmosphere. We all worked together, felt strongly motivated to do an important job responsibly, and rejoiced that Col. Dooley, our only officer, was a benign, good manager.

The investigations undertaken by the office were thorough, at times extensive, and always fair. I remember cases of men sent to the camp for intelligence training who arrived with a recommendation for court martial proceedings on espionage charges in their file. After in-depth investigation, full surveillance and lengthy interrogation, Col. Dooley cleared some of them for very sensitive duties. We were delighted to learn later that a few of these men had distinguished themselves highly in the battlefield and had received outstanding recommendations and medals.

In front of the headquarters building, there was an artillery piece, and a tombstone with the inscription: "Here lies the Marquess of Queensberry, died December 7th, 1941." There was one instance when I knew the service was being used politically to pressure a prominent newspaper columnist who was considered to be "hurting the war effort."

The man's nephew had been assigned to our camp. Apparently, the young man had a history of kleptomania and had been observed and was caught repeatedly in the act of stealing. The journalist was discreetly alerted to a situation in which the extent of his cooperation would make a great deal of difference to the handling of his nephew's case and the reputation of his family.

But, beyond such rare instances, the fairness and sophistication of our section was impressive. Given the professed theme of the training activities, this, to me, was especially admirable and enhanced my respect for the mentality of the American Army.

In many ways the camp was very different from any other training center I had known. On the surface Ritchie was more like an international club than an army camp. Most of the trainees were fluent in German, French, Italian, and sometimes Japanese. Some had made their reputations as writers, academicians and intellectuals in their native countries or in the States. The recreation rooms resounded with classical music, and, across the road from the entrance gate was a real deli, serving salami, pastrami and corned beef sandwiches on rye bread. In those times when white packaged bread prevailed, our deli was an unheard-of luxury.

There were also so called "CSU" (Composite School Units), troops who roamed the camp in German and Italian uniforms and carried foreign weapons. The sound of rapid firing from the Italian high-speed machine guns resounded often through the area. These men represented enemy units; they all spoke German and Italian as well as natives would. An apocryphal story suggested that an Italian soldier had once mistakenly parachuted on top of Camp Ritchie and had immediately been given an American commission.

Before being allowed to graduate, each trainee was dropped some miles away from the immediate camp. He was given a French or German map with orders to follow some tracks; along the way he was ambushed several times; he had to find certain locations and return within forty-eight hours to a command post. The local population had become so accustomed to these strange creatures wandering around the countryside like lost souls that some of the farm boys would accost them, and for a nickel would volunteer: "If you have a German map, you go this way, if you have an Italian map, that way, a French map, the other way." So much for intelligence security!

There was a small lake and a building that served as movie house and concert hall in camp. Eventually I gave some concerts there. The soldier in charge of the hall, who made all the "No smoking" announcements, was the then Corporal Bill Warfield who later became a well-known baritone and acquired international fame for his singing of "Ole Man River" in the movie *Showboat* He helped Andy learn how to swim in the lake.

There could not have been a more congenial environment for expatriate me; Marie, Andy and Laurie were safely ensconced in Waynesboro, a few miles away. Most of the time I was permitted to go home at the end of the work day, and, had it not been for the world situation, Hitler, the war, my parents' unknown fate, the complete uncertainty about what the next day might bring, life could not have been more agreeable. There were even a few old friends from Vienna passing through the camp, so that we had the company of familiar faces. As I was part of an investigative unit, I reported directly to our CO, Col. Dooley, was relieved of most of the usual army routine, and had almost complete freedom of movement.

Occasionally, there were pangs of homesickness for New York; especially when some secret orders came across my desk assigning men to the "Manhattan Project." Those lucky devils, I thought, sure that they were going to spend the war in Manhattan! It was not until years later that I learned about the secret atomic bomb work in Los Alamos that had been designated the "Manhattan Project."

With their War Department connections, the camp leadership tried to get the best possible people to service their camp. As a result, when a prominent Washington, D.C. chef faced army assignment, he was approached discreetly and asked whether he would mind being stationed within easy commuting distance of his home. And, if he did not object too strenuously, he was promptly shipped to Ritchie to make his contribution to the war effort in our mess halls.

One Thanksgiving day, Marie and Andy went to strenuous efforts to prepare an expensive meal. Working with a coal stove, they had to lug coal up and down stairs to heat the oven for a splendid turkey; I invited a few buddies to share a festive home meal. What Marie could not have known in fact, I hadn't known it, was that accumulated PX funds had gone to preparing a fabulous feast for lunch at the camp. A specially printed menu listed the gourmet delicacies served including oyster dressing and all kinds of other irresistible goodies, desserts, trimmings, etc. When the guests and I showed up at five in the afternoon for the festive dinner an exhausted Marie had prepared with great effort and finesse, we could barely look at the food without feeling sick. Miraculously, our marriage survived.

These pleasant experiences may suggest that assignments to Camp Ritchie were soft, cushy ways of avoiding combat. Many graduates ended up in very hazardous frontline assignments resulting in a high number of casualties. At the time of the Battle of the Bulge, many untrained headquarters people were hurriedly shipped straight into combat to bolster the endangered lines, with ensuing considerable loss.

The public often connects military intelligence with "spying." In fact, it includes the gathering of information from all available sources to assist in making command decisions. Actual "spying" behind enemy lines was handled during World War II by the Office of Strategic Services, the OSS. Ritchie trained linguists, writers, broadcasters and others in the interrogation of prisoners of war, liaison with foreign government structures wherever American troops were, interpretation of photo and terrain intelligence, the understanding of the enemy's order of battle and such related functions. Assignments ranged from frontline units to Supreme Command Headquarters.

Our office was charged with seeing to it that men trained at Camp Ritchie, mostly foreign-born, did not include real or potential enemy agents. A hostile agent assigned to Allied Headquarters and privy to planning and operations could potentially inflict immense damage to the war effort.

While we were there, it was wonderfully easy duty, especially in view of the tremendous sacrifices made by the troops invading Europe, or hopping from island to island in the Pacific. Apparently, our team at the post intelligence office must have done something effectively enough so that the decision-making powers kept us together until the war in Europe ended victoriously.

I would be dishonest were I to suggest dissatisfaction with having survived the war in Europe without seeing combat. My need to prove my courage and heroism was easily overcome by my wish to survive. Had I been placed into active combat, I can only hope that I would have performed adequately. I shall never know; yet, the mere fact that I have to write it this way implies to me that there must be reservoirs of guilt that I am struggling against. Rationally, at least, I have no regrets. I doubt very much that, could I replay those years, I would sincerely want to be sent into combat.

Once the war in Europe was over, the need to keep our team together ended. One day, I was summoned before a panel of about eight high ranking officers who interviewed me in colloquial, fluent German. Afterwards, I was asked whether I would volunteer for a special, then secret project, that would involve work with German prisoners of war, mostly members of Rommel's Africa Corps. I would be sent for some special training, and then have some input as to the region of my assignment. I volunteered enthusiastically, and soon thereafter was assigned temporarily to Fort Slocum, N.Y.

The project was highly classified because it was counter to the letter of the Geneva Convention on Prisoners of War which the Germans, in this special aspect, had violated all along. Specifically, it was based on the reasonable premise that returning prisoners of war, who had spent long periods of time in the U.S., would be considered experts on America by their neighbors, families and friends in hometowns and villages. Therefore, it became important for future policy decisions Germany might make in peace and war that the returnees form favorable impressions of America. We hoped that they would acquaint themselves sufficiently with our history, traditions and system of government to find them worth emulating. Short of this, we wanted them to be sufficiently impressed with the size, power, resources and strength of the United States to discourage any aggressive actions their government might contemplate in future years. I considered this concept very sophisticated.

To achieve these objectives, a bilingual specialist was needed to work under the Assistant Executive Officer of Prisoner of War Camps in implementing the various intelligence, education and propaganda functions required.

We were to be oriented to the project by attending a week's training session at Fort Slocum, near New York City. Forced to leave my family with indefinite plans until further decisions would be made, I reported to Ft. Slocum where exciting and stimulating seminars and training sessions took place. The group of volunteers represented a bright group of well-educated, European-born officers and enlisted men, who went through intensive reading and indoctrination concerning the various opportunities and problems this experiment might present. At the end, as promised, we were given a choice of regions among the various major prisoner of war camps. Never having been West, and eager to avoid the South, I applied for Camp White in Medford, Oregon, and was accepted.

Full of fantasies involving the Pacific, white-capped mountains, and ripe apples and pears, I was put on orders to Florence, Arizona. Questions about the geographical discrepancy between Oregon and Arizona were answered by referrals to the need for secrecy surrounding the assignment and the fact that prisoner-of-war camps in Oregon were under jurisdiction of the Ninth Service Command in Arizona. Off I went, provided with the luxury of a private roomette on the cross continental trip. Secrets must be well protected.

On my arrival in the Arizona desert, in a prisoner camp housing the most fanatical of Nazi officers in the Africa Corps, I discovered that nobody seemed to know what to do with me or a few others from the Slocum contingent. The intelligence officer and the assistant executive officer were in Los Angeles for a week's leave and nobody in personnel had an inkling of any reassignment for us. We were left alone for a few days to wait for our posting and given passes to visit Phoenix and Tucson. Eventually, we were put on orders to various military police posts in the West, all totally unrelated to our project. At this point, things were beginning to become critical, as we knew that, were we to leave, it would take the army forever to unravel the resulting confusion and get us to our assignments. We decided to sidestep the sacred channels of communication and walked straight to the office of the Commanding Officer. He was in on the "secret" and managed to get us to where we were supposed to be in the first place.

Camp Florence was situated in the middle of the desert, baked by a relentless sun. There were a few adobe houses and the camp itself, consisting of a large tent city for the prisoners and barracks for the American personnel. Most of the American quarters had an ingeniously rigged air conditioning system consisting of burlap bags in a box. Water was run through the burlap through a hose, keeping it wet. A fan behind the contraption sucked in the hot dry desert air, which, as it blew through the bags, turned cool and made the sweltering heat somewhat more bearable.

The German Officers continued to complain about the climate. The fact that it was close to impossible to escape from the camp did not endear it to them either. All shoes issued to the prisoners had a wedgelike marking on their soles. As soon as a man was missing, an air search would reveal his tracks in the sand. It was rumored that escapees would be given a few days to walk away from the camp until a jeep was sent out to escort their walk back.

While I was waiting for my assignment to be clarified, the first newsreel photos arrived which were taken by American troops who were liberating Nazi concentration camps. These horrifying films, showing the skeletons of the barely surviving living corpses and picturing the inhuman conditions in the camps, were later shown all over the world. After all the rumors we had heard, they presented the first visible proof of the almost incredible ferocity and cruelty with which the Nazis, under their barbaric extermination policy, had tortured and killed civilians, most of them Jews like myself and my parents.

I felt numb as I sat through the films. I absorbed what I saw; yet, I could not react emotionally. I could not reach for tears, or explode with rage. Some of that came much later. Then, all I could manage was to watch it all as if the atrocities on the screen could not directly affect me, as if I were watching a motion picture that portrayed events as part of a staged story. The film showed American soldiers escorting some of the inhabitants of a town bordering a death camp through it. When I heard and saw them all protest their ignorance of what had been going on under their noses, I felt like laughing in disbelief.

When my group came out into the desert air after the showing and we recovered our capacity to speak, we all felt that we needed to talk about what we had witnessed. In spite of all good intentions, though, we did not succeed in airing or sharing our feelings in any depth. Perhaps what we had witnessed came too close to be allowed to surface.

Most of us had relatives who, we feared, had been killed or tortured in one of these camps. The horrors we had watched came close to cutting past a threshold of emotional control. None of us could risk an explosion there and then; so we held on tightly and did not allow for anything that might have shaken our rigid defenses. We quickly resorted to our intellectual resources and our specific mission.

We agreed that it would be important, and much in line with the objectives of our "intellectual diversification program" (the official classified name for our project) to let the German prisoners see the films, and attempt a sample survey of their immediate reactions. The camp leadership agreed.

During the next twelve or so hours, working without interruptions and with the help of a few of the civilian typists at the camp, we produced a German translation of the English sound-track. As we had taken turns at writing out the German version, we arranged with the projectionists that we would take turns reading the German soundtrack. Whenever the original English soundtrack would come on, we turned down the sound, and read our German version through a microphone that carried it to the loudspeakers in the hall. In this manner, we were able to show the first concentration camp films to all the German prisoners of war in Camp Florence, Arizona, within 48 hours of the pictures' arrival.

As the prisoners emerged from the film, some of us, with

prepared, improvised questionnaires, asked their reactions. The results surprised us. We had expected shock, denial, excuses. Perhaps we had even hoped for some signs of guilt, remorse or revulsion. What we got, instead, was suspicious disbelief and accusations that the Americans had rigged these pictures for propaganda purposes. The only expressions of regret and pain came from those who complained about the "terrible cruelty" of the liberating troops who had forced their innocent mothers and relatives to view such inhuman sights. How could the allies be so ruthless and traumatize civilians in such a manner? "How dare they do this to my mother?"

Maybe we should have known better than to be surprised. Had I already experienced my professional training in psychology I could have predicted their reactions.

Medford, Oregon, came much closer to my fantasy image of that part of the country than I could have hoped. I saw the majestic, snowcapped Siskiyou Mountains and all the fruit trees I had anticipated; a pleasant aroma of fresh wood and wood smoke from the timber processing plants that abounded in the town was always present. Camp White was a few miles away in what was known as "The Agate Desert," so named for the semiprecious stones that were found there. It had been a major training camp, housing many thousands of soldiers in the recent past. Now, most of it was closed down, with the exception of an area that housed prisoners of war, mostly Africa Corps. More recently, less fit, very young, quite old, and poorly trained soldiers Hitler had been throwing into combat towards the end of the war were added.

As soon as I reported in, I contacted my immediate boss, a young officer who had been a journalist in civilian life, and requested some time off to find quarters for the family. In a relatively short time I located a pleasant apartment with cherry trees in front of the windows, for an affordable price, so I was able to send for Marie, Andy and Laurie. They embarked quickly on a strenuous cross country trip, spent mostly, I learned later, sleeping in baggage cars.

It seems that the train was overcrowded with troops transferring from Europe to the Pacific. However, reasonably comfortable space could be found in the baggage car where Laurie had been quartered. The men adopted Marie and Andy over the long trip, outfitted the baggage car with blankets, fetched food and drink, and helped walk Laurie. They also taught nine-year-old Andy how to play poker, and escorted him on frequent trips to the "men's room." Altogether, they helped make an arduous journey bearable.

Lt. Fahey, my immediate boss, was one of the three people who knew why I was there, (the others were the commanding officer and the intelligence officer). He made it very clear that he would give me a free hand in carrying out the designated project and would support my efforts to his best ability.

With some trepidation, I finally entered the stockade. No arms were permitted inside, and any American soldier entering had to turn his nameplate over at the gate, so that a search could be instituted quickly for anyone who did not return.

Some changes had taken place since the war in Europe had ended. Before then the camp had, at times, been under a reign of terror by active Nazi elements. There had been incidents of kangaroo courts that had condemned men found guilty of disloyalty to death. Executions were carried out by drowning them in toilets. Circumstances were not helped by the generally low quality of officers who had commanded prisoner-of-war camps. These officers were often on punitive assignments after having been found wanting in other commands. They tended to be pleased by the excellent morale of their prisoners, admired their marching and drilling discipline, and loved the anti-Semitic and anti-American songs the POWs chanted in harmony while they were marching, although they had no understanding of the words nor of the mockery the Germans were engaging in.

Much of this had changed in the two or so months since the war in Europe had ended and word of Nazi atrocities had filtered through. Yet, I was fearful when I first entered the compound and was introduced to the German camp speaker and his assistant. The speaker, who acted as leader of the camp, was a master sergeant;

his assistant, as I soon found out, was the real power behind the throne. He was a brilliant young corporal who spoke fluent English. I was introduced as someone who would be helpful in easing the prisoners' transition to civilian life in post-war Germany.

I had finally encountered "the enemy" in the flesh. I was asked some time later whether I had ever felt any divided loyalty between my new homeland, the U.S.A., and these men in whose language and culture I had grown up and lived until only a few years before. Without ever a moment's hesitation, I could answer that such feeling or thought never entered my mind or heart. I was an American soldier and they were the enemy who had not only fought against my country, but who had terrorized me and my family and my friends. If any other feelings were there, they were, initially at least, feelings of rage and bitter hatred. Later, as I began to work more closely with a staff of POWs, I began to see the individual human beings under the uniform. Once that happened, it was no longer possible to hate all of them; they became people, some of whom I could even like and admire. But that took a while.

Some miles away was a smaller compound, an "Anti-Nazi Camp," that held approximately a hundred German prisoners. Any prisoner who could reach the gate and let the MP guard know that his life was in danger from other prisoners was immediately whisked away to the "Anti-Nazi Camp."

I saw a golden opportunity for the first part of my plan. I knew that I could not begin my work until I had removed the most aggressive and menacing Nazis. Special camps had been set up which served to hold the most rabid Nazi prisoners. My first task, then, was to find the most vicious and active Nazis in the main camp and arrange for them to be removed to one of the special camps for the active Nazi leadership.

Under the guise of interviewing men to update their files on vocational and professional skills, I met with every one of the anti-Nazis. Routinely, after talking with them about their work experience, I initiated the subject of their transfer from the main camp. Soon I would come around to ask whom they considered the most threatening and fanatical Nazis there, and invite them to report their own experiences with such people.

After that, things became simple. I was under no obligation to build a case for a trial and did not need to present ironclad proof. If a name came up three times or more in different interviews, that man went on the list of those to be shipped out. After I completed interviewing everybody in the anti-Nazi compound, about 300 men were sent to an active Nazi camp. While we could not hope to have removed all the leaders, we could proceed with further educational programs without the risk of seeing our efforts frustrated by terror tactics.

The time had come to work on my project. Among the things that I hoped I could achieve were English language courses taught by English speaking POWs with the help of prepared plans that we could provide and supervise. I wanted to choose an elite group of prisoner-volunteers and give them a course in American history, based on materials provided by my project headquarters. I also wanted to work towards publishing a prison magazine, prepared by POWs under my supervision. These, and a number of other similar goals, I accomplished.

I knew that I needed the help of a staff of reasonably bright and reliable POWs in order to get started, so I tried to get to know some of the men. Finally, I settled on Karl Heinz, the assistant to the camp speaker, as my main helper. We had several long talks, and I was able to persuade him that this was a critical time for the future of Germany. He agreed that the choice lay between following a course to integrate Germany into the family of Western nations and their system of government, or to turn Germany into an agricultural nation in line with the suggested "scorched earth" policy of the Morgenthau plan.

Once we reached an understanding that his collaboration would be in the service of his patriotism, he became a loyal and helpful assistant.

Our relationship never became a truly personal one. I appreciated his intelligence and loyalty, but the wounds of my recent experiences with Germans had not sufficiently scarred over to permit self-disclosure. I did not wish to discuss my life, my background, my parents or my Jewishness with the "enemy." He knew I had lived in Vienna where I had studied. Beyond that, I did not invite or respond to inquiries. I believe that most of my fellow refugees in the U.S. Armed Services felt similarly.

There even was a joke about the American refugee soldier who was interrogating a prisoner from his hometown in Germany, and was affecting a strong American accent. The end of the lengthy interrogation came when the "American" asked: "Whom were you working for before you became a soldier?" and the German answered: "For your gracious father, Captain Cohn."

In trying to estimate the political composition of the camp population, Heinz and I arrived at similar figures, concluding that about ten percent were active political Nazis, about five percent were active anti-Nazis, and about eighty five percent were followers who would sail with the prevailing winds. The anti-Nazis were mostly religious Catholics, some Social Democrats, and a handful who had run afoul of some of the Nazi powers in the camp and were afraid for their lives. Our target population was the eighty five percent who were not deeply committed.

I initiated a series of other actions. Whenever there was an important political event in the U.S., I arranged that live translations of broadcasts by American leaders would be heard by all prisoners. Among the outstanding events were the speeches and explanations following our use of the atomic bomb in Japan. I translated the live broadcast of President Trumans's speech to the nation after the Japanese surrender. A series of excellent films were shown to all American servicemen under the title "Why We Fight." After my experience of running simultaneous German sound tracks with American films in Florence, I decided to show these five movies to all POWs. We arranged to get prints and prepared translations that some of my assistants and I read as the films were viewed by all prisoners. It took five or six showings to have the entire population attend each part of the series.

While showing one of the films, I had my sole war experience of feeling my life threatened by "enemy action." One of the sound tracks contained an overstatement. Describing the conflict between organized religion and the Nazi government, the announcer declared that all churches in Germany were closed, while the pictures showed church bells tolling and coming to a halt. The actual facts were that some churches had been closed in confrontation with the government, but not all. In working on the translation, this detail had escaped my attention.

Here I was, the only American soldier sitting in a large mess hall filled with about 400 prisoners of war, reading the passage I had prepared without suspecting trouble. Suddenly, the hall exploded in jeers, laughter and screaming, while a mob started to advance towards me. My heart stopped for a moment, I was covered with sweat, and I felt fingers of panic reaching for me. The few men of my POW staff gathered around me and quickly spirited me out a back entrance. I was completely unscathed, but badly shaken. Perhaps a small part of me felt somewhat gratified that I had finally tasted a measure of confrontation with danger.

After consultation with the camp powers, we decided that we would proceed with the films, but with more precise pre- planning. The watchtowers surrounding the camp, armed with machine guns, were alerted to pay special attention to any disturbance in the hall where the movies were shown. Somewhat frightened, I resumed my usual place near the projector for the next showing, my two or three assistants with me. As soon as the lights dimmed, a squadron of American MPs, armed with night sticks, quietly entered and formed a line in the back of the hall. Another squad took their places behind the screen. The time passed without any incident; I changed the offending passage and that was the end of the drama. I felt I had passed a baptism of fire, even though no shots had been fired.

In the course of one of the periodic shakedowns, when all prisoners were ordered out of their quarters and their belongings were searched for arms or suspicious articles, the MPs had confiscated a book covered with writing they could not decipher. It was the detailed diary of a German Africa Corps soldier, written in German shorthand. I had learned that same shorthand in school and was quite fluent with it. The document presented an opportunity to study the state of mind of a German soldier, as confided to a diary with virtual certainty that it would never be read by the enemy.

The diary was started long before the soldier's capture. He confided to it his thoughts and feelings at the time of capture and early imprisonment, his concerns about the war and the future of Germany. I spent some time dictating translated extracts which were then forwarded to Washington. There was great cruelty and righteousness in the description of some of the events and the discipline inflicted by the German prisoners themselves for the violation of rules; for example, a man was forced to stand thirty minutes on top of a table without headcover in the African noon sun for having swallowed more water than was allotted to him. In those days, long before My Lai and the Vietnamese war, I could smugly assure myself that American soldiers would never have resorted to such brutality.

Life in Oregon was exciting as far as my work was concerned. Andy loved the West and living conditions were quite acceptable. Marie had a job that, while not very satisfying, was tolerable; the surroundings were beautiful, and the climate, especially in Medford rather than in the hot camp, was lovely. Yet, with my European and more recently Eastern background, something was missing. People did not seem to relate as easily; it was more difficult to find congenial company, friends who would be interested in music, books, or politics. Everybody was friendly, but rodeos seemed to appeal more than operas. It was not a life style I was accustomed to.

I sang some solos for one of the churches and found everyone responsive and sociable. Yet, I felt an outsider. Somehow, I gained the impression that people tended to look towards the orient and the dangers it presented and that Europe and what it represented was very far away. In fact, it was. Marie encountered a bit of prejudice and anti-Semitism, not directed at her personally, but expressed in stereotypical generalities about Jews: "They are all wealthy, none of them work with their hands." Ironically and perhaps significantly, the people expressing such sentiments had never met, much less dealt with, any Jews.

Some of the lack of sophistication about European events was reflected in a fair amount of fraternization with prisoners who were on work details outside the camp. When caught with an American woman a German prisoner was punished, while his paramour was left alone. Punishment was usually a short detention in solitary confinement, and a close haircut, like those given to marines upon induction. I have no idea who thought up that particular form of discipline, but found to my astonishment that the loss of locks could reduce the toughest Africa Corps soldier to tears. So much for Samson and Freud's castration anxiety!

Some of the familiarity between American personnel and prisoners led to occasional security leaks. When the confidential orders for the shipment of radical Nazis were being developed, Karl Heinz, my assistant, sought me out and began to hint that something was on his mind. After some hesitation, he praised the importance of a former high school principal among the prisoners who might be of great help to any educational activities we might be planning. The man had been identified repeatedly as a fanatical Nazi, and, in fact, was scheduled to be on the next transport out. The camp apparently had some pretty well informed intelligence sources among the American staff. The illustrious educator went out on the next transport, and we were able to continue our project anyway. I never did find out how they knew.

There were also some minor jealousies among my American comrades. Because of the secret nature of my assignment, none of them really knew what I was up to, and wondered why I did not have to participate in some of the routine duties. I could not explain, and I suspect this did not enhance my popularity. As the translators of the intelligence staff had constant contact with the POWs, it was not surprising that they would gossip about the new man, and there was one proven instance of a spectacular indiscretion. All this added to my sense of isolation.

At Camp White a letter from my old friend George reached me. While stationed in Vienna, he had managed to get to Theresienstadt, also known as "Terezin," the Nazi concentration camp that had been "dressed up" for display to foreign countries. The Nazis had erected phony facilities and offered this camp as proof to the world that they committed no atrocities. When the Red Cross and other organizations sent representatives, they saw clean dormitories, decent food and children at play - for the duration of their visit.

There he had found documents attesting to my parents' internment for a period of time. My father had been assigned to duties in the post office, my mother had worked in the kitchen, and also appeared in a number of concerts and operatic performances that were being produced under the leadership of prominent musicians who were also temporary prisoners there. The records showed that my parents, as well as thousands of others, had been transported to Auschwitz, the extermination camp, on one of the last transports to leave Theresienstadt. It was obvious that they had met their death in the gas chambers there. In the years to follow, some of the few survivors who had been young and strong enough for forced labor and therefore able to escape the crematoria confirmed the circumstances of their murder to me.

For quite a while before then, I had essentially given up hope. Yet, I could barely fathom the final confirmation of their death. The knowledge struck me with the force of a deadening blow. The shock was so powerful that a wall came up between my intellectual understanding of this news and my emotional reaction that now all was lost. I had failed my most vital and important task. Now, in some way, all my strivings for survival seemed empty and meaningless.

The evening of the day I received this news, as if another me were operating, I supervised the distribution of the "Fragebogen," the political questionnaire that all Germans had to fill out. All that I remember is the helpless confusion between my wanting to kill and my certainty that that was senseless, and that short of my being severely provoked, I could not even muster up feelings of powerful hatred for these run of the mill, ordinary men before me.

The war had come to an end and my side had won. I, the soldier, had survived unscathed; my parents, the innocent civilians, had been murdered viciously. The time had arrived to pick up my honorable discharge from the Armed Services of the United States, and to go home as a civilian.

We packed our belongings. After a brief stay at a California camp, I was processed out of the army; I met the family in San Francisco for a glorious day's stay, and spent the night at the apartment of a hospitable stranger whom they had met on the train and who had insisted that we stay with her. On our last day, Andy managed to make one last leap from our stoop in Medford and sprained his ankle. So, with him limping along, (Laurie had to stay behind for later shipment, as she had been ill), we entrained with half of the Pacific fleet on the way home to New York.

Given good fortune and my strong, persistent, overlearned push to survive against all odds, these almost three years of my life had provided good seasoning. I felt I knew much more of my country and its people; I had a more realistic sense of where I might belong, as well as of the limitations that my early roots imposed on me in my aspirations to become one with the "natives." I had failed in rescuing my parents, but I now had my own family and I felt ready to start all over again, perhaps not quite at the beginning.

IX — "BACK TO SQUARE ONE?"

New York in the fall of 1945 was brimming with discharged and returning soldiers. The air seemed loaded with excitement and anxiety, a pervasive sense of tumultuousness. A lot of people, not only I, did not know where the next few years, the next few months, the next few weeks even, would toss them, yet they felt the relief of the survivor and the optimistic hope of the young.

The government granted all honorably discharged servicemen twenty dollars of unemployment pay for fifty two weeks, the notorious 52-20 club; this was a safety net of sorts if things did not work out right away. In addition, the G.I. Bill of Rights promised to provide generous help towards further education and training.

This enabled me to enlist the help of the American Theater Wing, an umbrella organization of people in the arts and entertainment. If you qualified in terms of your prewar experience, and passed a selection committee that found you sufficiently talented to merit support, you could use the G.I. funds for private, individual tutoring, coaching, or any art-related training. A faculty chosen from the finest professionals that New York had to offer was ready to work with you in their specialty if they found you acceptable. The government footed the bill, while the funds were administered through the American Theater Wing.

Except for the remainders of my accent, I no longer felt the green refugee immigrant, and, I was young and healthy. I also now had the support of my new family, in many ways an enormous boost; in others, a grave responsibility. It helped to be able to feel one of many. Although misery was not necessarily made easier by company, it was not the same as it had been when I was a penniless refugee. I was penniless again, but now I was one of the millions who walked the streets with a discharge button on his lapel. Somehow I felt more legitimate.

We stayed in a cheap apartment hotel on the West Side,

registered Andy in a New York school, and I had my olive drab army overcoat dyed black. Then I was off, trying to find a job, hoping to reestablish connections, auditioning wherever I could.

Fortune smiled upon me. Montreal, Canada, offered us our first chance. A Carol Grauer ran a rather elegant nightclub, *The Samovar*, in downtown Montreal. Carol was an unusual man, and the Samovar was an unusual club. He was a Romanian-born entertainer, a large, broadfaced man, bald and slightly effeminate, a bit in the mold of the actor Sidney Greenstreet. The Samovar was his great pride and he felt that the glory of his club was the entertainment he carefully and frugally engaged from New York.

His reputation had preceded him. He would engage classical singers, considered "promising," ballet teams, and a French-style "chanteuse" for each show. Carol was known to stop the show in the middle if anyone in the audience, sometimes after too much champagne, talked or interfered with the entertainment. With his inimitable accent, he invited the culprit to walk across the street to The Ritz, where he could continue drinking and talking without disturbing the marvelous show that Carol had imported from New York at great effort and expense.

He paid the same standard fee to all his singers. He provided for their fare; they could count on four to five weeks of employment as well as elegant meals at the club. I had no way of comparing his offer to prevailing fees; but when Carol, at one of his periodic audition trips to New York, offered me a contract, I was overjoyed and jumped at the opportunity. At this moment of my life the salary seemed a fortune.

Marie's parents kindly offered to see after Andy, who could not be uprooted again to another city; we still had Laurie's crate from her transport from Oregon, and so off we went with her to wintery Montreal. We found a delightful furnished room facing Mount Royal, within easy walking distance of the club and my short, but rewarding new career as a nightclub performer was started.

Carol generously lent me a white dinner jacket and helped me put together an "act." The audience responded favorably to my renditions of songs like "Yours Is My Heart Alone," the

"Toréador" song from *Carmen*, "J'attendrais," some Cole Porter songs, some Viennese songs such as "Vienna, City of My Dreams," and other semiclassical repertoire selections.

Marie and I had a good time there. I received fine reviews and I even appeared in a full page caricature of the cast; the other performers were good company and thoroughly professional artists, Montreal offered an exciting crunchy winter landscape, and while we got to bed late, and slept late, there was still time to explore the city and absorb its flavor.

It was not what I hoped to do for a living as time went by, but as a way of reentering a civilian existence, and as practice to earn my livelihood through my voice, it was wonderful. When it was over and we returned to a cold New York that seemed especially dirty after the permanent snow cover of Montreal, the end of December felt rather grim. Again, we settled in an inexpensive small hotel room on West Seventy-Third Street. Both of us had caught a cold, we had no friends in New York, and on New Year's Eve ushering in 1946, we huddled together, listening to a rented radio in our room. It was not a happy scene.

1946 began with a whirl of frantic activities. There were so many things to be attempted and so many goals to be achieved. The highest priority, as it had been through my entire adult civilian life up to now, was some way of providing financially for at least a minimum standard of living. After that, came the preparations for retraining and continued work on voice, coaching of operatic roles, stage deportment and the acting aspects of my operatic repertoire.

This was to be a time of testing for me. How long was it possible to maintain faith in my promise as a singer in opera and concert? Of the many auditions I experienced, each of which represented a trial of my talent and hopes, some, but certainly not all, were successful. Success could be measured in many ways. It could come as acceptance as a student, the offer of a job, a declaration of encouragement and advice for additional coaching and training, or the hope of future jobs, if and when a suitable opening might occur and more experience and study had been accomplished.

Then, of course, there were the many "Thank you, next please!" phrased in one way or the other. Depending on the degree of respect I had for those who were not interested in and therefore clearly not enthusiastic about the talents I had to offer, the rejections hurt and took time to recover from. So very much was riding on my hopes; a lot of reassurance and confirmation seemed required to justify the investment of time and energy in an attempted career in music, rather than in another, quicker road to financial survival. It was a much repeated truism in the world of opera that singing teachers, coaches, directors, agents, even public relations people in the field were earning a reasonable amount of money, while the singers themselves, except for a handful of stars, could barely survive. Perhaps this is true of all the arts.

When was I going to be able to stop being preoccupied with how I could survive; how I could succeed? Was the rest of my life to be involved with sole concern for myself and my family? Would there ever come a time when I could sense that I was giving something, contributing to others? My background had prepared me to fight for survival, but a part of me also felt obliged to consider others; it did not matter whether this would be in terms of social concern for those less fortunate, or by giving pleasure and gratification through the use of my talents. I had not entered medical school directed by the thought of acquiring quick fame and fortune. Would I ever be able to "give back" rather than be solely preoccupied with "what is in it for me?" At this moment of my life, I could ill afford such distractions. All I felt I could do was to store such sentiments for a more propitious time.

I did succeed in interesting some wonderful, knowledgeable people in working with me. Max Rudolph, later artistic administrator of the Metropolitan Opera, consented to coach me in operatic repertoire. A tall, handsome man, Germanic in style, with a slightly severe expression, he turned out to be a confidence-inspiring, exacting and experienced teacher. Maestro Rudolph, (nobody would ever address him as "Max,") wrote a definitive text on conducting and eventually became the music director of the Cincinnati Symphony. As artistic administrator of the Met, he acquired a reputation for correctness, combined with a determined refusal to commit himself to casting decisions. An apocryphal story went around that one of the leading artists running into Rudolph backstage said to him: "Nice day out today, Maestro," to which he was reported to have answered: "Sorry, I can't commit myself."

I learned a great deal from him; at one point, with the endorsement of the Metropolitan Opera, he sent me to Ettore Verna, then highly respected as an Italian singing teacher, to study the role of Scarpia in *Tosca*. Verna and I did not get along, but I continued to concentrate on the study of the role with stage directors and Italian coaches. Marie claimed that in the period of six months while I was training to be a villain, I was impossible to live with. Sadly, I never had the opportunity to perform Scarpia on any stage. As so many other things I aspired to, this, too, may have to wait for another incarnation.

Among other wise teachers and coaches was Joseph R. Rosenstock, soon to become director of the New York City Opera. A short, fair-skinned, handsome man, he had extensive conducting experience at the Met and abroad. He, too, was somewhat German and authoritarian in a benign way. He was also enormously knowledgeable and eager to impart what he knew.

His conducting style was at times referred to as "air-conditioned," because he noisily inhaled and exhaled while swinging his baton. He was courting a young soprano at City Opera; the story went around that he had taken her out, escorted her home, and at the door, in preparation for an affectionate parting, had responded to her primly addressing him as Maestro with: "My friends call me J.R.," whereupon she was rumored to have answered: "Thank you and good night, Junior."

Then there was Leopold Sachse, formerly General Director of the Opera House in Hamburg, later stage director at the Met, and eventually at City Opera. He was a tall, elderly, thin, very heavily accented walking encyclopedia of opera. His head was finely chiseled and he had a very loud, dramatic voice. Having grown up in a tradition of stage directors bellowing at singers and actors, he was quite baffled when American singers reacted to his shouts with bewildered shrugs of amazement and the comment: "Why is he screaming?"

We got along very well, and I learned much from him, first in private lessons, and later, when he directed me at City Opera. At times it was convenient for him to come to our place for my lessons. At one such occasion, the superintendent ran up to Marie and asked whether he should call the police. All these sounds of shouting and fighting were coming from our rooms. We had been working on Scarpia!

The G.I. Bill of Rights, through the American Theater Wing, paid for all these lessons. It also provided for coaching with Trucco, Toscanini's assistant conductor, on Italian repertoire, Thomas Martin of City Opera on French roles, and Leo Taubmann, perhaps one of the three top accompanists in America, on concert repertoire.

Beyond these marvelous training opportunities that came my way, life continued to make its accustomed, more prosaic demands. The hotel we first lived in decided on a "no dogs" policy, so we moved to furnished rooms on West Seventy-Third Street. There was just about enough room for us, a donated upright piano, and an improvised kitchenette.

We enlisted the help of Marie's family to place Andy in a private school outside the city. As much as we regretted having to separate from him again, our lifestyle, with the need to be available for out of town engagements and the mean smallness of our quarters left us little choice. We needed to find a more stable place for him where he would not be at risk of being relocated every few months. We hated having to do it, but, given our circumstances, we saw no other way and were grateful for the family's assistance that made it possible.

By necessity, we had to concentrate on paying the bills and keeping our bodies housed and fed. Church jobs, temple jobs, club dates, show jobs, announcing in German for Voice of America Broadcasts, even modeling assignments and small, accented character parts on the new TV shows; nothing was too small to be attempted. Some efforts proved reasonably successful; with others I just got by.

To obtain these engagements, it was necessary to make the daily rounds of agents, managers, producers, and to read or sing for auditions; all of it consumed a lot of time that had to be stolen from memorizing and studying the repertoire that my coaching lessons were to prepare me for. There was always the hope that I would walk into a producer's or agent's office just when they were desperately looking for someone like me. This did not happen often.

I did however succeed in landing two more substantial engagements. One was at the Papermill Playhouse in Millburn, New Jersey. An old paper mill had been converted into a charming theater where various musicals and operettas were performed in repertoire, each show running for a few weeks at a time. For two weeks I played Captain Lutte, a stereotypical German Cavalry officer in Noel Coward's *Bittersweet*. I not only killed the leading man in a duel eight times a week, but also sang a number praising the virtues of good Tokay wine. Noel Coward knew how to write spirited music, even if he was no master of writing for singers.

While the music was less than enchanting, it was wonderful to be on stage with a professional company, to sing and act, to learn stage-fencing from an expert in staged duels (it came in handy later when I sang the commendatore in *Don Giovanni*), and to collect a few weeks of regular pay. It was very hard work and quite exhausting; a lot of energy had to go into the commute by subway, ferry and train. On matinee days, in addition to singing and acting in two performances, I was also rehearsing for the next show, Sigmund Romberg's *New Moon*. The cast was young and glad to endure. On the way home, around midnight, we spent the time waiting for the ferry across the Hudson at the old Hoboken Clam House. We drank our beer and ate steamed clams with as much broth as we liked, and, as tradition required, we threw the shells on the well sanded floor. When I finally arrived back home, I whistled Siegfried's call from Wagner's Götterdämmerung loud enough for Marie to hear and send the dog down, yet softly enough, I hoped, not to wake the neighborhood.

A major excitement that year was my engagement as soloist with the New Orleans Symphony for three of their pop concerts. In addition to solo pieces with the orchestra under the baton of Jaques Singer, I was scheduled to sing duets with Susanne Sten, a delightful singer and musician, and the wife of my teacher and accompanist, Leo Taubmann. Susanne had a fine mezzo voice, strong, dark features, high cheek-bones and a gentle sense of humor. We were both able to smile at the "pearls of wisdom" that we produced for our press interviews.

All of it was an entirely new experience for me; my first solo appearance with a major orchestra, my first visit to a segregated Southern city. The contract called for what seemed, at first blush, an almost astronomical fee. It took a while to figure out that, after my agent's commission, my fare to New Orleans and back, hotel expenses, orchestra parts, posters and publicity materials, I came home with less than ten percent of my contractual pay. Yet, I was fortunate that this was an orchestra concert; had it been a recital with piano accompaniment, I would have had to pay the fee, and expenses, of my accompanist as well.

The price an artist had to pay for being a featured concert soloist was the assumption of responsibility for all expenses directly related to the solo performance. A fee was agreed upon; out of which everything not routinely supplied by the producers had to be paid by the performer. That included all orchestra parts or arrangements not in the orchestra's library. When the performance was part of a production (opera, oratorio, broadcast), such details were arranged and paid for by the sponsoring organization.

I learned how to rent orchestra parts for a symphony orchestra, and to discover where I could find scores that were not readily available. For my program, I chose some Cole Porter, Gershwin, light opera and Viennese songs for encores. I had the almost unbelievable nerve to disregard my Viennese accent to sing a

"Negro" spiritual type number, the popular "Shadrack, Mishack and Abednigo," in New Orleans. I even got away with it, and was applauded. Fortune must smile on the reckless.

The hall was very hot and humid, (weather had forced a move indoors), and it was not easy to keep the rivers of perspiration out of my mouth while singing. Yet, we received warm applause and excellent reviews.

It felt grand to get a taste of being a celebrity; newspaper and radio interviews, photos in the papers, reading one's inanities quoted. This also meant being taken out on the town by local board members, guided through New Orleans at night, having nightclub bands stop their playing to welcome the "celebrity guest"; it all seemed, and in fact was, quite unreal. Didn't they know that I could barely afford the price of my hotel room, and that I had no idea where and when my next "major" engagement would be? My appetite for further such engagements was certainly whetted. Unfortunately, they were not easy to come by.

Then, and I think now, there existed a class of young artists and singers who were broadly categorized as "promising." Unless they had family money, or other sources of income, there was no way for them to earn more than the barest livelihood through their talent. Yet they had to learn to present themselves for their engagements in the guise of being highly successful professionals. Why else would the public pay a lot of money for tickets to hear them? Managers knew that they could engage these artists at almost any price they chose, as the young "hopefuls" needed the experience and publicity so badly that they were in no position to negotiate for fees. The closer engagements were to important centers like New York, the more glamor they offered, the less they paid. In one year I had my picture on the music page of the *Sunday Times* on eight different occasions. In that same year I earned about $4000. from my singing.

The biographical sketches in printed concert programs give the insider in seconds a sense of the real level of success the artist has achieved. As a rule of thumb, the shorter the biography, the more prominent the performer.

Yet I loved these orchestra concerts in spite of the split personality they imposed upon me. When there were other singers involved, as in oratorio or concert performances of operas, the focus on one singer was not as intense as when one was the solo performer or one of two. In any case, it was thrilling to stand before an orchestra, and/or a chorus, and to feel the many eyes and ears directed expectantly at me.

A coach once described a singer in front of an audience as someone facing a thousand or more enemies who were ready to pounce on any weakness or error and devour their victim. It was that very challenge for performers to make the public their own, and to turn their audience's hostility into admiration, applause and "love," that created first stage fright and then, with success, a wonderful rush of adrenaline and exhilaration. The sense, perhaps the illusion, of holding that great monster out there applauding you in the palm of your hand contributes to the willingness of performers to endure the hardships of striving for a show business career. That flood of excitement, that "high," counts for much more than any monetary rewards ever could. It helps if one is able to afford it.

To my delight, I was engaged repeatedly to appear on the WOR Opera Hour. This was a nationwide broadcast that the Mutual Broadcasting Company supported every Sunday. More than 230 stations carried it. A large symphonic orchestra, conducted by Sylvan Levin or Emerson Buckley, usually opened with a prelude. The format then called for one of the two guest soloists to sing a few arias, followed by the other singer doing the same, after which the program concluded with a duet.

Most of the singers were young members of the Metropolitan Opera and I felt flattered to be engaged and reengaged. Among my partners were such artists as Jeanne Madeira, Claramae Turner, Ellen Faull and others. We met for an orchestra rehearsal at the Broadway Theatre Studio, and went on the air live, in front of an audience, two hours later. The artists as well as the conductors were a great pleasure to work with. As this was not a commercially sponsored program, the same fee was paid to all singers. We all got fifty dollars per broadcast from which we paid our agents' commission. But the applause was wonderful.

Over the next few years I had a number of solo engagements with various orchestras. I sang the Beethoven Ninth Symphony with the New Jersey Philharmonic Orchestra, the Verdi Requiem with the Westchester Symphony; later came Telramund in a concert performance of *Lohengrin* in the company of Blanche Thebom, Ramon Vinay, and other Metropolitan Opera stars with the Indianapolis Symphony under Sevitzky, and eventually I appeared in several concerts with the Philadelphia Orchestra under Eugene Ormandy; one, as Faninal in a concert performance of *Rosenkavalier*, another as Father in *Hansel and Gretl*, while already an intern in psychology.

In between, I sang a large number of oratorios with various choral societies who engaged me as bass soloist; included were Yiddish versions of Handel's *Judas Maccabeus* and *Samson* at Carnegie Hall; an orchestra concert in which I sang the opening aria of *The Flying Dutchman* at the Metropolitan Opera House; appearances as soloist with the Liederkranz Society at Town Hall; in Tanglewood, singing an English version of Moussorgsky's "Songs and Dances of Death," and others. I even performed a concert of quartertone compositions at New York's Town Hall.

Among the many funny or peculiar experiences connected with these performances, two stand out: One concerned the concertmaster of a well known orchestra who approached me at intermission of a rehearsal to say: "At the entrance in the beginning of that section, would you please turn in such a way that I can see your mouth; the conductor doesn't know how to cue us in, so I shall see to it that we follow you."

The other, in a very different vein, was Maestro Ormandy turning to the cast after the first piano run through of *Rosenkavalier*, saying: "Ladies and Gentlemen, I see you know your parts; please disregard me during the performance; the orchestra and I shall follow you."

Two opposing forces were pulling at me throughout these years of a "budding" career. One was the old familiar sharp-toothed need to earn enough money for me and my family to stay alive. It was always there, gnawing at me, and it was closely tied to my self-respect and to my hopes that I might succeed in my artistic aspirations.

The other was tied to the whole slew of activities that were to prepare me for a career as an opera and concert singer: All the lessons in singing, coaching repertoire, stage-direction, and all the "prestige" engagements that were accepted at little or no compensation, mainly for the purpose of furthering my experience and reputation. In both areas there were periods of highs and there were conspicuous lows. It seemed almost impossible to reach some acceptable balance.

Among the most exciting, productive and successful times were those spent singing leading roles at the Tanglewood Music Center under the direction of Boris Goldovsky, the engagements at New York City Opera, first in supporting roles and as understudy, later in leading parts; my New York recital debut at Town Hall, and the recognition that followed that performance.

The most painful times came in 1948 when I had contracted for an engagement beginning in the fall. The show I was in, *My Romance*, had closed prematurely in May; I could not accept work extending past September 1, and I was too late for any summer stock engagements. While out of town with the show, (we had opened in Boston, and had gone to Chicago before the planned New York opening,) we spent all the money we earned on hotels and meals. Marie had garnered a small part in the show, and was on the road with me. We arrived in New York penniless, with little chance of finding a way out. The bitter taste of finding my pockets empty, and of walking long distances because I did not have the nickel for subway fare, has never left my memory.

During that long summer of 1948, some of my income came from conducting survey polls for a marketing organization; I was allotted a certain area of city blocks, and my job was to try to get people to give me ten or so minutes of their time to fill out a questionnaire about their newspaper reading habits. I was paid per interview.

Another bit of income came from an engagement as soloist for a Welsh Music Festival in Pottville, Chambersburg and other Pennsylvania Welsh communities. Under the guidance of a Welsh singing coach, Rhys Morgan, a man with a powerful voice, well known and beloved in the Welsh community, we rehearsed solo and quartet numbers in Welsh, with a background of a Welsh chorus. I cannot testify to the accuracy of my Welsh diction, but the audiences were very hospitable; they cheered and treated us to groaning boards of great food at their outdoor festivals.

Happily, I had found a place for Marie in the chorus that came with us. I hoped that this would make it possible to spend our wedding anniversary in August together. Little did I anticipate that I, as a "distinguished soloist," would be housed in an elegant private home with the other three soloists, while the chorus was quartered in a hotel in a different town. On our wedding anniversary, Marie was standing in the broiling sun, clothed in a heavy Welsh folk costume while the temperature reached more than a hundred degrees Fahrenheit, and sang: "Gaver when, when, when," while I stood in the relative comfort of a summer suit. Not for a long time after that excursion to what was known in music circles as the "outhouse" circuit (Flushing, Pottsville, Chambersburg), did I stop hearing about our Welsh adventure, and it was not in the most loving of tones.

Among the other engagements I picked up that summer was an appearance as Dick Deadeye in Gilbert and Sullivan's *H.M.S. Pinafore* at the Yale Bowl. The Shubert Brothers, who had produced *My Romance*, the show which had just closed, were involved as producers and had invited me to participate. The highlight of my portrayal was a lusty rendering of "For 'e 'imself 'as said it, and hits greatly to 'is credit that 'e his an Englishman, that 'e his---- an Englishman." Fortunately, my Viennese accent did not show while I was singing.

Another engagement came from an Hungarian manager whom I had met through the composer Robert Stolz who had been an exile in New York before the war. Mr. K. was about to produce a quickly gathered stock performance of Strauss' *The Gypsy Baron* and wanted me to perform Zsupan, a pig farmer, father of the heroine, who was the character and comedy lead. The money he offered was too little, even in my impoverished state, but when I suggested Marie for a small part and chorus, we came to terms.

I returned home, holding the sheet music for the chorus in my hands, gave Marie the good news of her new engagement, and informed her that she was to report at three for rehearsals at Nola Studios. It would take many pages to describe the mixture of shock, excitement, anxiety, indignation and need to respond to challenge that followed. She did show up at the rehearsal.

The other soloists were quite good, although the conductor, who shall remain nameless, was unable to keep count and gave cues only to the "ballet" (one dancer.) As Marie knew how to open her mouth on time, he advised the rest of the chorus: "Pay attention to Hecht. She is the only one who comes in on time!"

We opened in Seacliff, Long Island, and after a few performances, saw that we easily outnumbered the audience. This, too, was a new experience for me. Mr. K., however was able to arrange for a "benefit" performance of our production at Carnegie Hall; I cannot recall for whose benefit it was supposed to have been. But here we were, happily singing and acting to a reasonably full house in what could only charitably be considered a professional performance.

At least, my father-in-law had the satisfaction of seeing his daughter in costume on the stage of Carnegie Hall. I suspect that he barely believed his eyes, nor could he have expected his son-in-law, the promising young opera star, to rhapsodize about his love for pigs and pork.

As an epilogue, Mr. K. did not show any intention of paying us the miserly salary he had contracted for. It took the Small Claims Court to help us collect.

Much of show business in America was controlled by the Shubert Organization, headed by two brothers, Lee and J.J.

Shubert. They owned most of the theater real estate in all the major cities and also had a share in many productions. Legendary road companies of *The Student Prince* and of *Desert Song* were, under their sponsorship, traveling the byways of America and had given rise to many stories and rumors. The Shuberts had a reputation for greed and for sharp paternalistic practices. The English star, Beatrice Lillie, when asked what she thought about the Shuberts, was reputed to have said: "Which one–SH or IT?" In fairness, I had no experience with them that would have given me cause for personal antagonism.

J.J. dealt with the production end. In his office on Forty-Fourth Street off Broadway, adjoining Shubert Alley, two casting directors held court. Mr. Simmons, known in the trade as "Ma Simmons," pre-selected the singing talent, while Mitzi judged the acting abilities of the candidates.

Among the many "do or die" auditions I appeared in that year was one for them; that led to a meeting with J.J. and a contract for a Broadway show he was planning. *My Romance* starred the beautiful Ann Jeffries. It was based on the life of a turn of the century opera star, Cavalieri. The show had a romantic book and somewhat sentimental music. My part was that of an aged, frustrated German opera singer who had become a waiter. That meant that I would break out into operatic arias at the slightest excuse; my special hit was the first sixteen or so bars from Mephisto's "Drinking Song" from Gounod's *Faust*; I was applauded on that at most performances. I also had a song beginning with:"My wife's Wiener Schnitzel, it tastes so good..." which clearly established my character. In addition, I conducted all cast members who were not on stage at the time in a backstage rendition of "Auld Lang Syne." The show was to open for a tryout in Boston, and then on to Broadway. My salary was pretty close to union minimum.

The Boston critics liked the show. That inspired J.J. to postpone the New York premiere, and to take the entire production to Chicago for a glamorous opening of The Great Northern Theatre which he had just refurbished at considerable expense. I cornered

J.J. backstage and explained that my salary could not possibly support my wife and myself out of town; I also wondered whether he could not find a job for her with the show, as I suspected he would rather add another body to his payroll than give me a substantial raise. He asked a few questions about her experience, and I vaguely suggested that she had a mezzo voice and had done some acting in Europe. I don't think he really was deceived, but he said: "Let her read for Mitzi on Monday." Thus began my wife's real show business career.

Marie reacted to the news with clearly mixed feelings. The Sunday before her audition we were in a minor car accident which painfully bruised Marie's knee. The next day, while I sat outside, more nervous than I had ever been for an audition of my own, she, in pain but nonplussed, went in to read for the casting director. She was asked to read the part of a bitchy society woman, and as she tells it, the ache in her knee gave her all the reality she needed to sound just right. Next, Mitzi took her into J.J.'s office; she apparently managed to charm him, because he invited her to join the show the next week as an understudy and part of the ensemble. When she hesitated, because Andy was due to come home for Easter vacation, he offered a curt "either or," and it had to be "either."

If truth be told, Marie's "show business career" was a testimony to her grit, courage and, what in New York is known as "chutzpah," lots of nerve. In fact, she had a pleasant small voice, a good, though untrained natural acting talent, and determination enough to "fake it." She joined the show, overcame her stage fright, and managed to learn the lyrics to the ensemble songs in record time.

A moment before going on stage in Boston for the first time, the Irish wardrobe mistress took a good look at her and exclaimed: "Jesus, Mary and Joseph, you look like holy hell!" Infuriated, as she had no time to retort, Marie rushed on stage, did her part, and went back to settle accounts and tell the woman off. Bridget smiled and hugged her: "Honey, I saw that you had never been on a real theater stage, and I figured if I can get you mad enough at me, you'll forget about being scared."

We were still in Boston, when old man J.J. decided to give a party for all the women members of the cast, excluding all the men. Marie accepted, hoping for the experience of a lifetime, especially when the great mogul, after a pleasant, uneventful evening at his Ritz Hotel Suite, said: "I have a little present for each of you girls; Tony, please give the ladies their gifts." The boxes they all received turned out to contain the remains of the chicken dinner that had been served.

And so we opened in Chicago with a big publicity blitz. Chicago's most influential critic, Claudia Cassidy of the *Chicago Tribune*, notorious for her strong negative opinions, hated the show. Her review was enough to murder the box office, which gradually fell off. In May, Shubert closed the show and announced his intention to have it rewritten for a fall opening in New York. That, for reasons which will become obvious, signaled the end of our part in it. We returned to New York, broke but yet another experience richer.

Throughout 1947 and 1948, I engaged in a variety of endeavors to help ends meet. I played in training movies for the army, mostly in parts of accented enemy agents or officers; I sang "club dates" whenever I could get them, and even did some vocal teaching and coaching at settlement schools.

An audition for the New York City Opera Company led to a contract to sing the role of the First Soldier in Richard Strauss' *Salome* in addition to becoming understudy for the Baritone lead, Jochanaan. I was also to sing several performances of Monterone in Verdi's *Rigoletto*, a part considered a promising opportunity for a young singer with leading part potential. Thus, I found myself on the roster of one of the only two opera companies in the United States that played for more than two or three months a year, which had by then acquired some respectability as the number two New York Opera House.

In professional terms, this was a major step forward in spite of the incredibly low fees that were routinely offered. I could work with highly respected directors and conductors, and have the opportunity for exposure to major New York critics. I jumped at the chance.

It felt great to be a member of a regular full repertoire opera company, to be listed among their principal singers, to have access to all rehearsals and performances, and, not the least, to discover the full greatness of the *Salome* score. While I was at an entry level in the company now, my colleagues treated me as a peer, and there was hope for future important roles. In fact, I did return a few years later in leading parts.

Back stage at the opera offered its share of amusing experiences. The general manager, Laszlo Halasz, a conductor of Hungarian birth, was a rather elegant looking man with a Mephistophelian expression who had served as model for quite a few of the less than flattering Hungarian jokes. In many ways he was a superb administrator who was known, if he found it convenient, to engage two different singers for the same role in the same performance, and then, just as likely to pick a third one to really sing it. This gave him not only a choice of the best one available but also conveyed to every singer to what extent he or she could be replaced on a moment's notice. In a very quiet way, he promised the moon if it suited his immediate purpose, and was not overly concerned about keeping his commitments. Given the operatic situation of all supply, and practically no demand, especially among younger singers, he usually managed to get away with it.

On one occasion, a stage director with a heavy German accent and a very loud voice was upset that one of the singers had not appeared on time for rehearsal. After ten minutes he threw a temper tantrum, declared that he could not and would not work under these conditions of lack of respect, and shouted so loudly that he was going home that he could be heard throughout the building. He was putting on his overcoat when the general manager opened the door and asked quietly: "What is it?" "Oh nothing!" came his meek answer. The coat came off and the rehearsal proceeded.

While "Maestro" Halasz was an excellent musician and coach, his conducting skills were not up to par. He was known for the "spoon down beat," meaning that when his arm came down, it was never possible to be sure when it reached the bottom, signifying the beat, because he immediately raised it, as if spooning soup from a pot. Sometimes that caused pretty confusing moments in the orchestra and on stage.

All in all, the engagement was a thrilling, exciting, at times frightening adventure. It contributed to my stage experience, and to my becoming better known to the powers that mattered in the music world.

A chance incident set in motion a series of events that ultimately redirected my life. After one of the many small concerts I participated in, an acquaintance came backstage to express his appreciation. Frederick Lechner was a German- born singer and a refugee who was singing leading character roles at the Metropolitan Opera while also functioning as Cantor of the Central Synagogue, a well known Reform Temple in New York. He complimented me on my performance, inquired about my career aspirations and my current situation, then asked, why, given the well known vicissitudes of a singer's existence, I had not considered officiating as Cantor during the Jewish High Holiday Services, reminding me that such opera stars as Richard Tucker, Jan Peerce and Robert Merill were singing cantorial services.

I explained to him that my knowledge of Hebrew was quite limited and that I had no background or preparation for what he suggested; he offered to teach me in less than three hours what I needed to know. I challenged him on that score; he accepted my challenge, we met, he showed me the music he was using which included the English transliteration of the Hebrew text to synchronize with the score, and I was on the verge of a new venture that was to have an important impact on my future.

Once I realized that it would not only be possible, but quite easy, to acquire the necessary skills to officiate at reform services, I had to confront myself honestly. Over the years I had sung in choirs for many Jewish holiday services as well as for church services. In the ensemble, I performed anonymously, often behind a curtain, usually under the direction of a choir conductor or organist who was responsible for all preparations. I was hired for the part my voice would take in the music, much as orchestra players would render services through their instruments as part of a combined effort.

This undertaking was fundamentally different. I would stand in front of the congregation, robed, filling the shoes of a minister, a member of the clergy, acting in the Jewish tradition as the "Sh'liach Tzibur," the messenger who would convey the prayers of the faithful. I would be fully responsible for the music, with the organ and the choir taking their cues from me.

I knew that I was ready musically and vocally to take on such a mission, but I had to resolve serious internal conflicts first. I had to question myself as honestly as I could about my ability to officiate at services without feeling like a hypocrite or an actor, leading the congregation in prayer. In spite of all possible and tempting inducements I was not prepared to treat cantorial work as an acting part, as I might when I sang the role of the High Priest in *Samson and Delilah*. In some way that I did not fully understand, I sensed that respect for my parents and my Jewish inheritance was involved and that, even without being aware of any fear of divine wrath, I could not violate these traditions.

I did not believe in a personified deity; I could not accept the notion of a kind or stern father figure watching over me. Yet, I was able to feel fully the emotions of awe, respect, and hope when dealing with the unfathomable mysteries of life and death. The dread of the unknown, the unpredictable, the uncontrollable, was very close to the surface of my feelings, especially when the means of expression relied on music rather than on the relatively inadequate language of words alone. I was moved by the poetry of the prayers to be chanted; while I was not quite prepared to be called "Reverend," there was reverence in the acceptance of my human lack of omniscience and the fear of the forces that affected me without my ability to understand or control them.

I was very sure in my identification as a Jew. Although I grew up in an assimilated environment, there was never a question of my Jewish roots and how they had shaped the lives of my parents and grandparents. The tradition of temple music had been part of my early years, and I had much admired the Cantor of the synagogue I had attended as a boy. I felt quite capable of drawing on my thinly covered memories of traditional Jewish songs and tunes.

But my knowledge of Hebrew was, at best, sketchy. I had not had the sort of religious education that would have equipped me to read from the Torah; my adolescent rebellion, compounded later by my bitterness over the fate of Jews, most specifically my parents, had imbued me with a sense of resentment against formal religion.

I wanted to be as sure as possible that my decision would not be over determined by rationalizations about convenience. Yet, the prospect of earning a decent fee by the use of my talents, as well as the opportunity to test my ability to provide an emotional experience to a congregation and myself, entered into my considerations heavily. For the moment, I only had to decide whether to attempt this new venture for the High Holidays; I could postpone all future plans until after that.

I told Lechner that I would try, if he would help me with selecting the proper material. He consented, recommended me, and, almost immediately, I received an offer to perform services for the Reform congregation in St. Paul, Minnesota. I was offered a generous fee plus all expenses, including first class train fare.

X — "O LORD, I'M ON MY WAY..."

My stay in St. Paul gave me great pleasure and gratification. I was treated as an honored guest, housed in an elegant apartment hotel, and, for every evening of my two-week-stay, I was entertained for dinner, and at times for lunch, by the families of the congregation. Evening services were held in the municipal auditorium to accommodate the large crowds; morning services were at the Temple. Collaboration with organist and choir went most smoothly; Rabbi Saul Applebaum, a gentle, warm man with a wonderful sense of humor, and his wife, received me graciously. I was able to speak openly to him about my lack of experience, my aspirations in concert and opera, and he, in turn reassured me and calmed my anxiety.

The congregation responded enthusiastically to my work and invited me to come back the following year. I returned to New York enriched emotionally and monetarily. Beyond the delight I felt about the cordial reception I had received, I truly enjoyed the respect afforded me. As an aspiring artist, one tended to be treated somewhat akin to a jobless bum between engagements. ("What are you doing next?" "Mm, Mm, I am negotiating for a possible concert next month... Mm Mm.") It felt awfully good to be admired, not quite in the "star treatment terms" of concerts, but with honor and appreciation. My appetite for more was whetted.

Over a cup of coffee at the Rabbi's house:

Rabbi: "Fred, help me understand something. Here, you are doing a splendid job; the chanting sounds great, the people love you, and, above all, clearly you are having a ball. We have spoken about some of the hard times a young aspiring singer goes through. So tell me: what stops you from doing some cantorial work in the New York area; make it a little easier on yourself and your wife?"

I: "Look Saul. Next year I am going to be thirty years old. Over the last few years I have worked very hard at preparing myself for a career in concert and opera. I have been encouraged and have had some minor successes. I am not ready to throw in the towel and settle down to something that I certainly have enjoyed doing, but that I cannot see as the end of the road for me, an activity that until a very short time ago was not even part of my dreams."

Rabbi: "Who's talking of 'ends of the road?' I have in mind your approaching certain large synagogues who can afford to have a 'full time Cantor,' meaning that you would sing services Friday night and Saturday mornings and holidays. They would be fully aware of your aspirations and take pride in having as their Cantor a man of such potential fame. Look at Tucker, Peerce and the others."

I: "So where do I find these places that are dying to pay me a salary while I pursue a career?"

Rabbi: "Funny you should ask. I happen to know of three temples in the Metropolitan area who will have a vacancy for a Cantor next season. I would be glad to write them about you so they could at least audition you. You too could write them, refer them to me, spell out your ambitions, offer your services and see what happens."

I: "Sold!"

He wrote, I wrote, and in the early spring of 1948, I auditioned for the largest reform temple in New Jersey, located in Newark for almost 100 years. Soon I was offered a one-year contract to participate in all services as the Cantor of the congregation. My salary was nominal, but steady, and provided for a reasonable standard of living for a full time job. It was understood that my duties would not include anything not related to the musical portion of the religious services, and that I would be free to pursue

other activities as long as they did not interfere with my contrac
tual commitments. I was to begin September 1st, with a widely
publicized installation service.

So there it was, signed and sealed. For the first time since I had
left the army, I could count on a regular pay- check and could look
forward to a long term engagement. There was some trepidation;
I could detect the rumblings of fear deep in my stomach without
even having to pay special attention. But, and it was a big "but,"
there was also great excitement and anticipation. In my preparations I found that I loved much of the music and looked forward to
performing it. All I had to do was to survive the summer until my
contract began.

After the installation ceremonies, attended by more than 2,000
people and broadcast locally on radio, life settled down to a routine
of holiday, Friday night, and Saturday morning services, with my
commuting first by railroad, later by car, from and to New York.
Beyond that, though, a lot of things changed fundamentally.

No longer were my energies and anxieties absorbed by concerns
for material survival; the pressures of these extremely urgent
stresses, I believe can be fully appreciated only by those who have
experienced them. It took a while to accept the certainty that next
month's rent and food bill would be paid without my hope for some
quasi-miraculous event. It took getting used to the reality that we
could now concentrate on building a possible career; no longer
were we forced to accept any offer that came our way, no matter
how absurd, just because we depended almost literally on every
penny we could earn.

I also had to become accustomed to wearing custom-made
clerical robes, chanting from a pulpit and being addressed as
"Cantor" or "Reverend." I reassured myself that I was not being
hypocritical, that I did not and would not profess to any pretense
about who I was and where I stood. Furthermore, the response of
the congregation readily convinced me that I was fulfilling the task
for which they had engaged me, to their complete satisfaction.

We managed to settle down in our new situation. I took some private Hebrew lessons, and eventually became a charter member of the American Conference of Cantors. My association with the temple lasted more than ten years, by which time the needs of the congregation had changed and so had mine. They were about to move to the suburbs and wanted a Cantor who would participate in religious education and community efforts. I had acquired my Ph.D. in clinical psychology by this time, had begun psycho-analytic training and felt that my life was taking new and different directions.

There were a number of highlights in my cantorial career. I introduced a large quantity of contemporary music, including the service by Ernst Bloch, and compositions for Jewish services by composers primarily known for their secular works, e.g., a Kiddush in Jazz style by Kurt Weill. I was able to curtail the use of some of the musically dreadful, yet much beloved compositions that had been created early in the century in an attempt to imitate the style of Protestant Churches. Also, I was enabled to commission works by lesser known contemporary composers for special occasions. With relatively little rumbling the congregants supported these innovations. As I had no aspirations beyond maintaining a high level of performance and of musical quality during services, I had no problem keeping myself out of internal temple politics.

Some parts of the ritual touched me deeply; I especially remember the "aleynu," the adoration chanted towards the end of all services. The congregation and clergy rose and faced the ark while I pressed a button that activated a motor which over twenty or more seconds slowly opened large and heavy bronze doors to reveal the scrolls of several Torahs. Their ornate mantles and silver decorations were brightly lit against a white silken background while I intoned: "Let us adore the ever living God..." The sole-mnity and awe of the moment never failed to send shivers down my spine. During holiday services especially, many such moments occurred and moved me deeply.

Then, in contrast, there were some of the Saturday morning services in the huge sanctuary, attended by ten or so older ladies who cherished meeting their friends and were prepared to suffer through the chanting if it had to be, even though it did interrupt their conversation. I well remember the drives through tunnels and bridges in the midst of Friday evening rush hour to get to Newark in time for Sabbath Services. As our services were often carried by local radio stations, we had to begin on time. No matter how early I started out, it seemed almost impossible not to be hemmed in by other cars while traffic was at a standstill, the clock was ticking away, my heart was beating rapidly, the sweat was pouring down my face, and I felt completely helpless and trapped.

All in all, my ten years as Cantor presented a cherished experience. I have no way of speculating how my life would have turned out had I not had the opportunities this experience offered me. When Andy was married to the daughter of temple members, I officiated together with the Rabbi. In many other important ways my temple activities affected the course of my life; the events that led me to initiate and pursue that career change were fortuitous. Yet, I also knew that I did not wish to spend my future devoted to the routines that were part of a Cantor's life.

In 1949, a friend helped us to find a charming small garden apartment in a mews on the upper Westside of New York. This was our first chance to have our own apartment, our own inexpensively acquired furniture, and some space for Andy to sleep when he came to New York. Marie fashioned a coffee table from a painting which she mounted on the legs of a cot; we started with some mattresses and box springs, and, for the first time in our life together, felt we had a home. In those days of rent control the monthly cost was only slightly more than the cost of our current garage bill for three days. As time went by, we were able to buy our apartment as part of a Coop, and furnish it somewhat more generously; we are still enjoying it many years later.

While I was settling down in my cantorial work, I continued studies in voice, repertoire and stagecraft. I even acquired a manager who was able to obtain occasional engagements. One

Saturday, following services, I received an urgent telephone call from Marie. Mr. Lustig, the manager, had called. I was to proceed immediately to Radio City Music Hall, ask for Mr. Page and Mr. Leonidoff, the conductor and stage director respectively.

Radio City was doing a half hour segment of Bizet's *Carmen* four times a day, and the baritone singing "The Toreador" had lost his voice. I was to do a quick audition and to take over that evening.

Somewhat out of breath, I sang for Page and Leonidoff, and was hired, and, before I had time to catch my breath, costume people started work on me to fit me into the matador's outfit, while Leonidoff explained the stage business, and Page informed me that I would have to memorize the English text immediately. In the meantime, reluctantly, he would permit me to sing in French, the only language in which I knew the role, while the rest of the cast and the chorus would continue in English.

The stage business was more complicated than I could have anticipated. Radio City Music Hall showed a first run feature film at every show, which meant that the acoustics in the huge house totally relied on a speaker system, and no sound could penetrate into the vast audience space without it. A row of five or six microphones were set among the footlights in front of the stage. This created a major problem. If the soloist stood too close to the mikes, his voice would go out above them without being picked up, and would disappear into the cavernous hall. Or, if he were more than four or five feet away from them, they also would not pick up the voice, and the same thing would happen.

The staging required a fair amount of interplay with the mezzo soprano who sang Carmen, as well as with some of the women in the chorus and with some of the women dancers. It also included some stage business with a rose in addition to extensive waving of the bull fighter's cape.

That evening, trying to control the tremor in my knees, I went on for the six o'clock show, and somehow managed to survive without wrecking everything. I sang in French while already thinking of the English lyrics ("Here's a toast, a toast to men of daring..."), trying to remember where I was supposed to be at any given moment, and to whom I was addressing myself; Carmen, the men of the chorus or the dancers offering me flowers. I could only hope, fervently, that my voice would not be above or below the microphone pickup zone. Anyway, the audience applauded.

After the first show I received a note from Mr. Page, informing me that he was happy with my singing, but would I please try to insert the English version at the nine o'clock show. I had to overcome what I later learned to call "negative learning transfer." Whenever I tried for the new English version, the well-studied French words came to mind and mouth. The second show was distinguished by the most amazing mixture of French and English words, interrupted at times by doubletalk sounds and nonsense syllables. There was no reason to assume that anyone in the audience knew the difference; they applauded anyway. I knew, and Page knew.

This too passed, and by the time the Sunday shows came along, matters were under control. I continued for another week and a half, until the program changed. Friday evenings, while I sang at the temple, a substitute from the chorus went on for me.

Radio City had wonderful dressing rooms. Mine was the size of a large living room, boasted a couch, some other furniture and a piano. In show business, there are either too many offers at one time, or there are none. During that particular time period I was also rehearsing for several other engagements; coaches came to my dressing room and used the piano there so that I did not have to leave for other rehearsals between shows. The schedule of so many performances a day was strenuous, but it also was thrilling to sing at the great Radio City Music Hall at Rockefeller Center.

Over the next few years, my career began a slow, but steady ascent. My engagements tended to be more important; I had more name recognition; the parts offered me were mostly leads; my singing and acting was reaching a higher level of competence and quality.

In the spring of 1949, I met and auditioned for Boris Goldovsky, known for his intermission programs during the broadcasts from the Metropolitan Opera. He was also a pianist, opera manager, stage director, and head of the Opera Department at the New England Conservatory and at the Tanglewood Music Festival, the summer home of the Boston Symphony Orchestra in the Berkshire Hills. He engaged me to do the baritone lead in the American premiere of Benjamin Britten's *Albert Herring* that summer, and to participate in other opera productions at Tanglewood. This coincided with my temple vacation time, so I was able to accept, and thus began my most important period of learning and growing in the world of music and opera.

Goldovsky was not only a Renaissance man with a huge body of knowledge in music, theater, the arts, opera, and history; he also had highly original ideas about staging and performing. Above all, he was a phenomenal teacher. During the following four decades more than three quarters of all important positions in the American world of opera were held by his pupils. That included stage directors, singers, educators and impresarios.

A slender, light skinned, blondish man in his forties, he spoke with a Russian accent that became more pronounced when he lectured in public and almost disappeared when he was teaching. He had a superb command of English, enormous charm, and a gift of establishing immediate intimacy with those with whom he was working. In contrast to most other European-born directors, he respected singers and invited them to use their own intellect and personal resources on stage. "Remember, you are not an idiot who can only open his mouth when a conductor points a stick at you," was his instruction. By helping "singing actors" delve into the background and past of the role, he enabled them to achieve a measure of authenticity that transmitted itself to the audience.

He came from a distinguished Russian family of artists, and loved to entertain his disciples with riproaring anecdotes about his Russian musician-relatives. He respected talent, and when he considered a performer talented, he adopted each one into his family. He lent his car if it were needed, shared meals, delighted in giving advice on musical as well as personal problems. When he engaged me to sing with his New England Opera Company in

Boston, he insisted that I stay at his house in Brookline.

It was not clear whether he cared as deeply about the people he worked with as he was able to convey to them. That was probably irrelevant; what mattered is that we all felt he did, and that made for an artistic environment in which creating and performing under his guidance became pure pleasure and led to constant challenging discoveries of hidden resources.

Marie and I fell in love with the Berkshires the very first evening we arrived by train from New York. It was a cool evening in late June. We were hungry and tired after a seven-hour ride when we checked into our rented quarters. In the hope of finding something to eat for Laurie, our canine companion, and ourselves, we walked a short distance to the then famous old Curtis Hotel. The well manicured, tree lined streets of Lenox, MA, bordered by magnificent looking former mansions that now had become schools and institutions, created an immediate sense of comfort and civilized hospitality. The barman at the Curtis, although ready to close for the night, managed to whip up some sandwiches and a soupbone; on the way back to our room we breathed the clean, wood-scented air and felt truly contented.

Tanglewood confirmed our first impressions. On the grounds of a magnificent former estate, the tall trees and cultivated lawns reflected decades of exquisite planning and care. The view south from the hill on which the administration building stood ranged over sloping meadows and a lake, called the "Stockbridge Bowl" to include the foot- hills of the Berkshires, reaching into Connecticut and New York State. Beyond its own beauty, the scenery brought back the lakes and foothills of the Alps, and reminded me with a warm surge of the glorious times my parents and I had spent on vacations in Carinthia. On the memorable occasion of Serge Koussevitzky's birthday, (Tanglewood was then his domain), the Boston Symphony played waltzes on these very lawns as we danced.

And so we began work, from nine in the morning to, at times ten, eleven o'clock at night, seven days a week. If we were not rehearsing, we were coaching with top accompanists, memorizing music, words and stage movements; or, we sat around with Boris, conductors, including at times Leonard Bernstein, and stage directors, and we discussed the operas we were rehearsing, or anything that related to them, their composers, or the world of music at large, including careers, staging, and singing. Sometimes, when the day was very warm, we moved rehearsals to the private beach Tanglewood maintained on the Bowl, and worked and swam there. A group of us arranged to rotate buying lunch for the entire cast in the morning so that we could eat picnic-style during a short break.

On those rare occasions when our schedule allowed, we attended concerts and rehearsals of the Boston Symphony Orchestra in the shed not far from our opera building. On the even rarer free evenings, we hitchhiked to nearby Pittsfield for a restaurant meal.

The other cast members were young, with some experience, many on the cusp of important international careers. In the Britten Opera other leading roles were taken by James Pease, Ellen Faull, David Lloyd, and Edith Evans; Rosalind Elias, Marni Nixon, Mattiwilda Dobbs and a number of future members of the Metropolitan Opera were among us.

Beside singing the American premiere of *Albert Herring*, I appeared in the role of the Count in a full production (costumes, scenery, orchestra) of the second act of Mozart's *Marriage of Figaro* and sang *Rigoletto* in a full production of the last act of the Verdi opera. All this was prepared and performed in less than five weeks.

Tanglewood had offered Marie a job with the Friends of Tanglewood, which entitled her to a pass to all events. We had a wonderful time, especially when my old friend George joined us as assistant conductor, and my old sponsor, Felix Wolfes, conducted.

At the end of Tanglewood, I dreaded the impending let-down which always followed the hectic excitement of rehearsals and performances. My dread did not last long, as I was invited to return the next year to sing the lead in another premier. This was to be the first American performance of *Le Roi d'Yvetot*, the *King of Yvetot*, by the French composer Jacques Ibert, the composer in residence for 1950. Of course, I was delighted to accept. Also, Boris engaged me to sing Onegin with Phyllis Curtin as Tatiana, in a production of Tschaikowsy's *Eugene Onegin* he planned for the New England Opera Theater during the next season at the Boston Opera House.

When the final curtain came down on the season, we all collapsed in a stupor. We needed a few days to unwind, preferably on the beach of the Bowl.

On one of these days, Boris, a young man and I were sunning ourselves quietly on a raft, floating on the water. Everybody in Tanglewood knew that Goldovsky worshipped Mozart with almost religious fervor. The unnamed young man decided that this might be a good time to test the master:"So what's so great about Mozart; at times I find him boring."While I held my breath, Boris slowly turned and looked gently at the questioner:"You know, if I were eighteen years old, and I would die to make an impression on my elders, that is exactly what I would say."The young man dove into the water, not to return to the float.

After our return to New York, and my resumption of services at the temple (my contract was renewed with a small raise), I began to receive more calls for engagements. One came from CBS. The network planned a television production of Verdi's *Traviata* four weeks hence, and I was offered a small part with the possibility that I might have a chance to cover the great Lawrence Tibbett who was to sing the leading baritone role of Germont Sr. They agreed this commitment would not interfere with scheduled temple services.

The entire venture became more and more exciting as we plunged deeply into rehearsals. The director, Herbert Graf, reputed to have been the original "Little Hans" described in Freud's historic monograph, was inspiring, as, in his own way was the conductor, Fausto Cleva. Cleva, a superb musician and conductor, had a well-deserved reputation for being extremely unpleasant. One of his favorite gestures, when he was not satisfied with the way a singer performed a phrase or made a musical mistake, was to shrug his shoulders, turn his head sideways and raise his hands, palms upwards as if to implore: "God help me, why do I have to work with these hopeless idiots, I give up!" This did not tend to raise the self-confidence of the poor devil on stage who, unlike the conductor, did not have a score in front of him.

Three days before the scheduled broadcast, it became painfully obvious that Lawrence Tibbett might be "indisposed." His voice had begun to give out, and rumors were abounding that he was drinking too much. I was told to prepare to take over if necessary, on three days' notice. All had to be kept secret, of course.

It was not easy to resist panic. Tibbett was, albeit ageing, the dean of American baritones, a great artist with a towering international reputation. His part in the first network opera broadcast had been widely publicized. I had studied the role of the elder Germont in the original Italian. Now I was given three days to restudy the part in the English translation, and to be prepared for the carefully mapped camera movements of the staging, to perform before an audience that might exceed a million viewers.

An assistant conductor, Walter Ducloux, was assigned to me; every moment I was not needed to rehearse my original part for which a cover was arranged, I spent being coached in another studio, while on call. My heart beats faster even now just recalling the anxiety of those days. On the one hand, should I be called in, I would be offered the legendary understudy opportunity that sparks movies; on the other hand, there was the nightmare of all performers: to be stuck during a performance, forgetting the words, missing the notes, making a fool of yourself and finishing your career hopes, all in front of a large, anonymous audience. An hour and a half before performance time, it was decided that Tibbett, who had sung the dress rehearsal quite adequately, would go on. With an overwhelming sense of relief, I sang my small part, an important experience richer. Mr. Tibbett's voice unfortunately cracked on the high notes of his aria: "Di Provenza..." At this stage of his career, he could afford an embarrassment much more than I could have at mine.

I felt a time for major decisions was coming close. As I approached thirty-five, three paths lay before me. I could go on trying for the brass ring, hoping that the odds would significantly be in my favor and that I could survive the emotional stresses of periodic defeat; I could throw in the towel and resign myself to the more or less comfortable subsistence as Cantor, adding some teaching activities; or, I could change directions altogether, protected by the safety net of my cantorial position.

XI — "ONE DREAM IN MY HEART, ONE LOVE TO BE LIVING FOR.."

As 1950 rolled along, my manager, my coaches and my singing teacher felt the time was propitious for a bold step forward; they agreed that I was ready for a New York Town Hall debut.

These five words by themselves may not mean very much. But, a New York Town Hall debut meant presenting oneself to the toughest audience in America, perhaps in the world, for an audition. Given my background at that time, I could count on coverage by the music critics of all New York newspapers who would weigh critically my potential as a serious singer. At that time, there were four major morning papers and four afternoon papers; none of their music critics were known to be gentle when it came to reviewing young singers who were bold enough to venture their debut in the Big Apple.

Good or outstanding reviews could mean a colossal step up the ladder to national concert tours and powerful impresarios; poor or average reviews meant pretty much that you had tried but had been found wanting, so good luck in another line of work.

Bad reviews could also seriously endanger my position with the temple. Members of my congregation could be counted on to pay special attention to the concert. I hoped that many would attend and knew that they would read the critics carefully. Thumbs down might have catastrophic consequences when contract renewals came up. This was another risk. Arrangements for a debut recital involved an immense amount of preparation and a not inconsiderable amount of money. My personal manager, who also had to be compensated, could arrange for the rental of Town Hall, preferably at the beginning of the season. A large number of routine matters consumed hundreds of hours of time and energy. Tickets and programs had to be printed, flyers prepared, ads placed; some publicity had to be arranged, press releases and photos had to be sent out, critics had to be invited, program notes had to be written and a myriad of other details had to be organized. If more funds were available, much of this could have been handled by paid specialists. In our case, we were barely able to scrape up the absolute minimum amount for the barest necessities.

These were just some of the administrative aspects of planning a debut. Much more important and challenging was the designing and preparation of the actual program to be performed. The pieces selected had to meet a variety of criteria. The program could not be too popular or "hackneyed" without inviting scathing comments from reviewers. It also could not be so esoteric that the non-musicologists in the audience would fall asleep. It should be creative, "different," interesting (giving the critics an opportunity to show off by writing at some length about the composition), and, above all, very much above all, it must showcase the artist's voice, musicianship, performance appeal, intelligence, and expressive talent at its very best. As the frank purpose of the presentation was to call favorable attention to the singer, these considerations loomed most importantly. For me, it was essential that I like and enjoy singing the numbers I selected.

A successful recital also required a reasonably full house. Not only did a large audience help to energize the performance, the entrance fees collected would, in a minor way, help to defray expenses. It was vital to plan the program to arouse the curiosity and interest of the public. All this required seeking counsel from experts, extensive research at music libraries and publishing houses, and, of course, reading through and experimenting with possible selections to determine their suitability for my voice and taste. In the era before copying machines, I had to negotiate loan arrangements for the music I wanted to try. It was important to devote part of the program to works of contemporary composers who might offer some unpublished manuscripts or possible premier performance of one of their songs. I visited a large number of composers living in the New York area, some quite well known. All were willing to see me and were eager to have their works performed in a debut. When I finally selected a number of singable, and to me, exciting modern compositions, most of which I scheduled for the last part of the program, I found the composers were eager to help coach and prepare me to perform their works. At times, it was not easy to reject some of the compositions that were offered without offending the composer.

Finally, I included in my program two first New York performances, among them, the powerful Creed of Pierre Cochon, Bishop of Beauvais, from Norman dello Joio's "The Triumph of St. Joan" which was singled out for special praise by the critics.

Once the program was selected, it had to be properly prepared, memorized, rehearsed, polished, and tried out. Leo Taubman, a marvelous pianist, accompanist and friend who had made his reputation by accompanying some of the most famous concert artists of the day, traveling with them across the United States, was unsparing with his time and energy. He worked with me patiently for hours on end to reach a level of performance that satisfied him.

During the summer of 1950, while singing the *Roi d'Yvetot* in Tanglewood, I was able to try out the entire program in the chamber music hall. I approached the first test before a live audience with great trepidation and was relieved and encouraged by their enthusiastic response. Their applause helped diminish the occasional panic-filled nightmares that preceded the concert date.

October 8, 1950, Sunday afternoon at three, was to be my moment of truth. I felt I had done all I could to be well prepared. My program included pieces in English, French, German, Hebrew and Italian; it ranged from songs of the early sixteenth century via Lieder and Ballads to modern compositions. It reflected accurately, I believed, the state of my skill and talent at that time.

The weather favored us with a crisp New York fall day. I was reasonably rested, and delayed our departure for Town Hall as long as I could to shorten the agonizing wait in the "green room" before facing the audience. We took the subway to 42nd street, and were met at the stage entrance by a frantic manager and a somewhat agitated accompanist. It was about seven minutes before three, and they were, to put it mildly, concerned.

The house was almost completely filled. The composers whose works I was performing were seated in the boxes to which they had been invited, in the event they were to acknowledge accolades from an admiring public. All the newspapers were represented; a large number of musicians and colleagues with whom I had performed at various occasions were part of the audience. I noticed, when I finally stepped out on the stage, that many members of my congregation had shown up as well.

As I had expected, in the last few minutes until the lights dimmed, I was seized by gut-twisting stage fright. Once I faced the applause of the audience, and felt the air charged with friendly expectation and excitement, the fear vanished, I began to enjoy myself and launched into Gluck's "Ode an den Tod."

Things seemed to go splendidly. Applause mounted from group to group of songs. The Dello Joio aria, the last piece before intermission, led to a real ovation, with Norman Dello Joio graciously sharing the audience's approval. Mr. Lustig, my manager, came backstage to congratulate me, and cautioned me to direct all offers or inquiries by other agents to him without making any commitments on my own.

And so it went right to the end; I was not allowed to stop until I had sung three encores. Of course, Marie and I were thrilled and riding an emotional high that almost, but not quite, balanced our anxiety over the impending newspaper reviews.

A friend was giving a dinner party for us at his house. We were planning to wait there until the early editions of tomorrow's newspapers were on the street. Everybody, I believe, knew that, while the audience response was encouraging, there was no predicting whether the critics would pronounce similar judgments.

Our concerns were unwarranted. In the early morning hours, somebody came in with the fresh papers. Exhausted and apprehensive, we rushed to the music page. The reviews were raves, exceeding all my fantasies.

The New York Times, under a large headline, wrote a subheadline that read: "Baritone, Who Has Performed in Opera and Radio, Heard in First Solo Program." The critic called it a "felicitous occasion," a phrase repeated in the following Sunday's *Music and Theater Section*: "...revealing a big, beautiful voice, got the best notices of the recitalists..." The review went from superlative to superlative, praising "startlingly clear diction...excelling when the music was of dramatic impact...(voice) boomed powerfully... musical intelligence...able to float attractive light tones..." I hardly could believe my eyes, as my heart skipped a few beats and danced wildly.

The New York Post mentioned "...resonant high baritone voice... assured stage presence...excellent musicianship...made an impression which was obviously superior and exhibited uncommon gifts...voice soared freely...sang throughout with keen appreciation of the musical and histrionic values under consideration..."

The New York World-Telegram and *Sun* wrote of "...a sturdy voice of marked resonance with a technique that watched over every note like a guardian angel...It was a pleasure to hear a voice as fresh and clear..."

Not in my wildest dreams would I have anticipated a reception of such unanimous approval. When we finally fell asleep that morning, exhausted and triumphant, it was with a sense of accomplishment, filled with the highest hopes. It appeared that we had risked, striven hard, and now could really hope for the rewards.

Things did not quite turn out that way. In many ways the debut pushed my career forward. I became better known and graduated from small parts to leading roles. Major impresarios expressed interest; they offered concert tours to small towns across the country. Yet, to sign up for these would have necessitated leaving my job at the temple. It was questionable whether the tours would have furthered my career significantly, and the financial rewards were minimal. I was not prepared to take that chance at this time of my life, and I still feel I made the right decision.

What would really have helped at this turning point was a reserve fund of $30,000 or thereabouts, or a patron of the arts who could come up with such a sum. Money was needed to finance exploitation of the excellent reviews we had received. An opportunity to build on the initial success by mounting a promotion campaign would have required retaining high-priced personal representatives, public relation specialists and top management. Several careers, based on critical success, took off when thus "properly exploited."

Money alone never would have been quite enough. There is an old show business dictum that there exists no "pull" between seven and eleven at night. It means that the public cannot be deceived when the actual performance is poor. There can be no substitute for talent. But, perhaps, neither talent alone, nor promotion and money alone can do the trick; both were needed.

Stardom can only be built on a foundation of talent, skill, personal appeal and magnetism, aggressive determination, *plus* a support system that can bring these qualities to the attention of a wide audience.

We had put all our energies and resources into preparing for the debut. Now that it turned out to be a success, we had "shot our bolt" and were no longer in a position to push further and capitalize on our achievement. There was all this bliss and excitement, but for us there was little to do but wait for things to happen and for Mr. Lustig, my agent, to become a magician.

A good friend who owned some movie theaters insisted on laying out a promotion sheet which featured highlighted reprints of the various reviews, headed by a quote from the *New York Times* in large type: "**A FELICITOUS OCCASION**." The last of our money went into having it reproduced. Ironically, none of us noticed that the word "felicitous" was spelled "*felicitious*" until it was too late to make any changes; so it remained.

The recital had apparently captured enough public attention to lead *Etude* magazine to commission me to write an article about it. I did so under the heading "So you want to give a Town Hall Debut Recital."

As time passed, I became increasingly sensitive to the ups and downs of my life. Teetering on a seesaw from great excitement and high hopes down to profound disappointments and self-doubts, and up again, began to exact its toll. Success might well be around the corner, but I began to wonder how long I could go on striving for it.

In the midst of all the tumultuous hopes, fantasies and activities, an occasional series of images intruded that shocked me because they seemed so far away from my present situation. In that scenario, I was a professional person, a doctor perhaps, who spent his days seeing patients, engaging in some research, going quietly from home to office to clinic. There was a delicious sense of peace and security about that portrait.

Joseph Rosenstock, who had been one of my coaches, became General Manager of the New York City Opera. They were about to produce Strauss' *Rosenkavalier* under his baton. He remembered me, I auditioned for the leading bass role, Baron Ochs, and was offered a contract for the part contingent on my ability to memorize music and text in the next three months. This was no minor condition, as the usual time to prepare this very long and difficult role was a year.

I had grown up with the opera *Rosenkavalier*, knew much of it as a listener, and had absorbed the Viennese atmosphere and dialect during my adolescence. I adored the marvelous character of Baron Ochs, immortalized by the great Richard Mayer whom I had admired many times in that role. The challenge was too tempting not to try. I signed the contract, and with the help of a conductor friend I spent every free hour during the next three months studying the music and text.

As always, when I approached a new role, I thought that I would never be able to learn it, but I also knew that eventually it would "become mine." So it happened with Ochs, an infernally difficult part, musically as well as vocally, and especially, dramatically. By the time I reported for rehearsals, about four weeks before the scheduled performance, I felt reasonably prepared.

Although it was something that I was not about to spread around, I also knew that, while I had all the notes for the part in my voice, it had been written for a bass. Mine was basically a baritone with low notes available. Long stretches of the role lay in a range that most comfortably would be sung by a bass who could count on more heaviness in that part of the voice than I could. I felt confident that I could sing a good Baron Ochs, but I also knew that I could not be a "great one."

As it happened, my performances were well received, praised by the critics, and I was engaged to sing the role for a number of performances in the following seasons. In fact, when the NBC Opera Theatre decided on a national television broadcast of *Rosenkavalier* in an English translation, I was engaged to switch roles with the baritone who had sung the leading character baritone role of Faninal and we both sang in a very successful production over national television. From that experience came a series of concert performances of the opera with the Philadelphia Orchestra under Eugene Ormandy, performances which to me presented the highlights of my career.

I was very lucky to be able to continue my cantorial work during all this. The absolute top fee that the New York City Opera paid singers at that time was $150 per performance. There was no compensation for rehearsals. Given the time spent on preparation and rehearsals, the limited number of performances during one season and the agent's ten percent commission, my operatic income barely covered the price of the coffee I consumed during rehearsals.

The performances brought me to the attention of one of Europe's most influential managers who had engineered George London's stellar career at European opera houses. He offered to arrange a series of auditions in Vienna, Munich and Wiesbaden, if I could be available to be in Europe for about a week.

Things really began to heat up. We were operating under a constant aura of excitement, anxiety, hopes, doubts and fears. I had to approach the temple for a week's leave of absence. In view of the fact that so many of my activities were outside of my job there, I felt considerable trepidation and some guilt, but, without question, I had to proceed. With some reluctance, I was given permission. Then, of course, I had to scratch up money for the trans-Atlantic trip and hotels in Europe.

I prepared carefully for the auditions. Once the final selection of pieces was made, I cut out the relevant arias and scenes from the piano scores of the operas chosen so that I could take them with me on the flight. I decided to open with the aria of the Count from Mozart's *Marriage of Figaro*. After that I would offer selections from *Tosca, Carmen, Meistersinger, Walküre, Rosenkavalier* and others. All of them were prepared in the original language; potentially a problem, for operas, except when they were performed at Festivals, were presented in German at Austrian and German opera houses. In addition to my American passport, I procured the special permit that would allow me to cross the Russian zone of occupation in Austria.

XII — VIENNA, FIFTEEN YEARS LATER

On a bright January day, I took off on a KLM flight in a propeller-driven aircraft to Amsterdam where I was to change planes for Vienna. The flight to Amsterdam took nineteen hours. I was so excited I could barely stay in my seat. This was my first return to Europe, and more specifically, to the city of my birth. Its name had turned to ashes in my mouth.

Of those first nineteen years of my life, eighteen had left me with warm, pleasant feelings; I was comfortable with myself; Vienna's cultural environment and education had shaped me. I loved Vienna and had been proud of being Viennese. And then, after the almost volcanic eruption of hatred and violence had taken their toll, I felt rage, grief, resentment and the wish to disown any connection with the city, its people; even its language. Yet, I could not expel the Viennese in myself: the memories, the music, the natural beauty, the friends, so much so that I had drawn heavily on that part of me for my career by portraying Viennese characters, and singing Viennese songs.

After I left Vienna as a penniless refugee in mortal danger, the Holocaust occurred and a horribly bloody war had brought conquering troops of four allied nations to restore some sanity to the old city. It now lay there, inert, expectant, bearing the scars of some bomb damage, some initial violence by the occupying troops and some deprivations. In 1952 it was ruled by American, British, French and Russian soldiers who discharged their responsibilities in an uneasy alliance. In a bizarre political twist encouraged by the Americans, the Viennese had succeeded in promoting their claim that they had been the first victims of Nazi aggression and therefore were entitled to special treatment. As a witness to the enthusiastic welcome with which Vienna had embraced the German troops, I could barely suppress my hilarity and chagrin at this revision of history.

So here I was about to return, an American with an American passport and money, possibly considering resettlement as a member of the Vienna Opera which I had idealized throughout my growing up years. My confusion was boundless. I had no notion of what to expect. What I felt was not really anxiety; it was a state of high tension, excitement; at times, numbness.

When we landed in Amsterdam at six in the morning for a short stay before boarding the plane to Vienna, KLM treated all transit passengers to a Dutch breakfast at the airport restaurant. Waiters in tails and white ties made a profound impression on me of postwar life in Europe as they served platters of cold cuts and cheeses.

Towards evening we began circling above the Vienna airport. My heart was pounding as I looked out at the dark and gloomy snow covered scene. All passengers boarded a bus to Vienna center, under the watchful eye of a British soldier with rifle and fixed bayonet who stood next to the driver. The bus passed some rather seedy outlying parts of Vienna under Russian occupation to reach the center which was under four-power rule; an armed member of one of the other allied powers provided official representation to prevent possible Russian removal of passengers.

We soon arrived at the inner city terminal. I changed some dollars into schillings at a favorable exchange rate and registered at the Pension Schneider, a place much frequented by guests of the Vienna opera. It was popular not only because of its proximity to the Theater an der Wien which housed the opera while the bomb damage of the Staatsoper building was being repaired, but also primarily because the proprietors, through special connections provided heat and an adequate breakfast. The familiar scents of Vienna, a special aroma consisting of a mixture of smoke from chimney pots, cleaning materials that smelled differently from those used in the U.S., coffee, and whatever else, overwhelmed me with nostalgic memories.

I dined at a restaurant which, even at a reasonable price, served the finest venison I had eaten since I left Vienna. And then, highly stimulated, I roamed through the old familiar streets, the

Kärntnerstrasse, the Graben. Everything seemed covered with dirty snow; the cold was penetrating. I passed a large number of prostitutes who, in my memory, had always patrolled these streets at night. There seemed to be more of them, and fewer potential customers. The women added a strangely erotic aura to the dismal, poorly lit streets.

For an hour or more, I wandered through the city, aware that I should be resting for the auditions that, after all, were the true reason for my being there. But I couldn't silence the hundreds, even thousands, of memories that crowded my head. It was as if every reminder of every moment I had walked by a particular building or down a street in my first nineteen years, converged on me all at once. These strands of different feelings and circumstances welled up at the same time, vying with each other to enter my consciousness and receive my full attention. Finally, physically and emotionally exhausted, I meandered back to my pension, took a sleeping pill and fell into a deep sleep.

The next morning, after breakfast, I was more solidly back in the present and began to make the necessary contacts. Time for a stage audition at the Vienna Staatsoper was arranged for the next day. A rehearsal of the audition material with one of the opera's assistant conductors who was to accompany me was scheduled, and life resumed a semblance of organized reality.

As the accompanist and I ran through the material I had prepared, with one important exception everything went rather well. For the first time in my professional singing life, I showed a tendency to sing slightly flat. Such a potentially fatal flaw upset me greatly, until I was told that the lengthy exposure to propeller noise could cause such feedback distortions for a short time. This stopped at the audition, the next day. At the time, though, it gave me a nasty shock.

When I was not busy preparing for the audition, I resumed my walks through Vienna and found that I had suppressed names of streets that had been thoroughly familiar. It took a while before I was able to recover complete recall.

I visited the house I had lived in most of my life in Vienna. It had not been damaged and looked quite respectable. Attempting to visit our old apartment, I knocked at the Super's door, and here she was, crying: "Jesus, Mr. Fredi!" I could not forget that this was the same person who had directed the stormtroopers to arrest me, and so I did not reciprocate her hearty greeting.

I went back to my elementary school and to my Gymnasium. It now was a special middle school for musically talented children. As I walked into the "aula," the hall next to the entrance, I felt transported back to the first day I had come here to take my entrance examination at the age of ten. The smell and ambiance were unchanged.

During my walks I spoke to everybody and anybody who felt like talking. As always, the Viennese were approachable and loved to chat. All of them confirmed my long held, somewhat generalized impression of what I had come to think of as the prevailing Viennese character.

People, on the surface, were charming, often somewhat submissive and ingratiating. Overtly, they, as I, had been trained above all to be "polite." They were able to convey to any stranger the impression that they felt honored and flattered by the opportunity to converse with such a highly respectable personage. As the conversation continued, it did not take special sensitivity to discover the underlying envy, self-pity, and rage, that, given a chance, could erupt in a destructiveness that had managed to shock even the German Nazis. I had been a witness to these eruptions and this knowledge hung heavily over my contacts with the famous "Viennese charm."

Much of this was concealed behind a certain geniality and an agreeable sense of humor that included an ability to laugh at themselves. A popular Viennese caricature was that of a bicyclist, bowing his head to those above him, and stepping on those below him. A certain servility permeated the manner in which anyone in authority was addressed. At the opera house, every director, conductor, or manager was followed by five or six flunkies who took notes avidly, and, at least in my view, kept bowing and scraping while repeating their superior's title. "Yes, Herr Kapellmeister," "Immediately, Herr Oberregisseur," "Of course, Herr Generalmusikdirektor." I had become accustomed to the informality and use of first names in the American theater, so I found this behavior pompous and repugnant.

When I eventually met a group of Americans living in Vienna, some of them former refugees who now worked in various American culture projects, I felt I could breathe some fresh air. The quick camaraderie, the almost immediate use of first names, all made me feel at home and gave me a sense of belonging; with even the most forthcoming Viennese, I felt I was a stranger.

In those days the Viennese were most afraid of the Russian "barbarians" whose conquering Siberian and Mongolian troops had raped and plundered mercilessly in the first weeks of the occupation. The Americans, French and English were "adored" as cultured saviors, and were envied, hated and despised for their power and wealth. An apocryphal story going around Vienna reflected some of these attitudes: The Russians were said to rape the women, the French seduced them, the Americans bought them, and the English married them.

As I wandered around, occasionally stopping for a cup of coffee at one of the coffeehouses, a passage from Schubert's song, "The Wanderer," kept running through my mind:

"The sun here seems to me so cold,
The blossom withered,
The life so old."

Ghosts of the past surrounded me; my wounds had not yet healed enough to make me tolerate Vienna.

One evening I bought a ticket to the Musikvereinsaal to hear the Vienna Philharmonic perform Beethoven's Ninth Symphony, conducted by the great Furtwängler. As I surrendered myself to the glorious sounds in the magnificent, so very familiar hall, I noticed that the slow movement became slower and slower. Suddenly, without warning, I saw the very tall and slender Furtwängler sway from side to side and collapse. As the players saw that their conductor was no longer leading, the orchestra slowly tapered off over a period of twenty seconds or so, while the audience gasped in horror.

After a short while an announcement was made asking the audience to stay in the hall while the maestro was recovering from an indisposition. He did not recover that evening and, after an hour or so, another announcement explained that the rest of the concert would have to be canceled. A few months later, Furtwängler died from a heart ailment. In some almost mystical, symbolic way, this incident reflected my feelings about my return to Vienna. There was something about the sudden, lightning switch from inspiring beauty and serenity to shocking tragedy that struck a responsive chord in me.

The next morning, I sang on the stage of The Theater an der Wien, where the Vienna Opera performed. An ongoing rehearsal was interrupted while the general manager and the leading conductors sat in the audience and some of the current stars watched me from the wings. For about twenty minutes, I was asked to sing various selections.

Afterwards, while some of the singers in the wings applauded and made encouraging comments, the general manager and Joseph Krips, the leading conductor, sat down with me. They complimented me, and told me some of the issues they wanted to discuss with my European manager. Ideally, they wanted me to make a guest appearance as Amonasro in *Aida* during this season. This would help determine the scope of my possible engagement as a member of the company. Short of that, they would consider an entry contract for a salary of about 100,000 Austrian schillings for the year. In U.S. currency that was approximately $4000.

They did not ask for an immediate reply, and wanted further discussions with my agent. I was in turmoil. That I was being considered, even for a guest appearance, with this illustrious company, boggled my mind. I was scared to death of the prospect, but also flattered and tempted by the chance; yet, I knew that I could not afford to leave my temple job for prolonged trips to Europe, even with all other things being equal, without seriously endangering my coveted life support.

Could I abandon the emotional and physical security I had

found in the States? Could I justify moving my family into an existence near the poverty line, in an environment alien to them in language and style? Could I tolerate living in this occupied city, performing for the people who had driven me out and killed my parents? Even, if all that were possible and I could overlook the reality that one cannot spend twenty-four hours a day in the opera house and must live among the Viennese, even if I were to take this gamble, what were the odds that I could establish a truly successful career here?

Even if I could rival the great George London in acting and singing talent, could I, a Viennese Jew returning from exile, count on the Viennese public to welcome me? There was nothing exotic about me, they knew "my kind," and had not been too well disposed to us in the past.

These and many other thoughts, questions and feelings were churning wildly in my head. I was grateful that there would be time to sort out matters before I had to decide. My manager informed me that there were rumors of a change in the artistic management of the opera, and that the famous conductor, Clemens Krauss, was mentioned as the new prospective head. To cover all possibilities, he had arranged for me to audition for Krauss the next day. Krauss was recording an oratorio with the Vienna Philharmonic at the Konzerthaus, the other great concert hall of Vienna, and had agreed to hear me during a break in the recording session.

Clemens Krauss had been director of the Vienna Opera in 1937, and I had heard and seen many wonderful productions under his baton. He was also a notorious Nazi in those days. Less than a year before the Anschluss, he had left Vienna for Berlin with his wife, a leading soprano, and a group of prominent singers. Their departure was to serve as a political demonstration against the then anti-Nazi Austrian government. Apparently, he had changed colors some time before the end of the war, because an intensive investigation of the denazification authorities had cleared him.

With all my reservations, I did not feel that this was the time to refuse auditioning for him. He listened attentively for about twenty-five minutes, then invited me to sit next to him while he commented in great detail on my voice, repertoire, and the direction he thought my career should take. He was very flattering, and warned me strongly against singing a Wagnerian repertoire too soon in my career, lest I strain my voice prematurely. He also suggested a series of parts, mostly in the Italian and French repertoire to give my voice a chance to develop and mature more slowly. To my surprise, the audition turned out to be an exciting and encouraging experience. He, did not however, become the next director of the Vienna Opera.

I spent my Vienna evenings attending performances at the opera. One was a memorable *Don Giovanni*, performed in German in the relatively small house by superb singers, with the audience responsive to every bit of humor. The other was *Traviata*, also in German, and it was one of the most dreary, inadequate and provincial performances I had ever heard. In the States such a performance would have been a critical failure in the smallest town. So much for the consistently high level of the Vienna Opera.

During intermission I ran into a woman who had been a colleague at the Gymnasium. I remembered well how proudly she, then seventeen, had displayed a concealed swastika when the Nazis were outlawed. Now she greeted me with warmth and affection. She and her husband, a high ranking civil servant in the Foreign Ministry, asked me to join them for a drink after the opera. I was flooded by a mixture of conflicted feelings. Undeniably, there was a certain nostalgia; shared memories of a time long gone when we had lived through many joys and stresses together as comrades; with it came a sense of rage, yes, even revenge for the hurt she and her Nazi pals had inflicted, some curiosity about what the years in between had been like for her and some other colleagues she may have been in touch with.

I accepted and had a glass of "Glühwein," a sort of grog-like spiced hot wine, with them. Irene entertained me with touching stories of the suffering the war had caused them. I heard all about the terror of the bombardments, the cruelty of the Russians, the shortages of food and fuel, and the arrogance of the occupiers. I also heard about how lucky I was to be living in America.

In the interest of peace, I hid my lack of pity and sympathy for her and the Viennese. I also did not express my gratitude that she and her friends had speeded my flight to the United States.

That night the sleeper to Munich was drafty, and lacking the glamor I had remembered from prewar sleeping cars. When we approached the Russian Zone which the train had to cross on the way to Munich, Russian soldiers boarded, and I was awakened to show my special passing permit. They looked very young, in their teens, and I was sure they could not read the passport; but they passed me on and I arrived in Munich somewhat rested.

The audition in Munich was handled by a local agent, and went smoothly without much comment. Further conversations were scheduled about a possible engagement.

I was impressed by the extensive unrepaired bomb damage to the city; I was also struck by the complex security measures surrounding the "Herr Generalintendant." Anybody who came to see him had to pass through a series of barriers and secretaries, each of whom checked on the visitor's admissibility. I was sure that the President of the United States was more easily accessible.

As the guest of the Herr Generalintendant, I attended a performance of *Aida* in which an American singer, a student of my vocal teacher, sang Radames, the tenor lead. Also featured was a new young soprano, Leonie Rysanek, whose star quality performance signaled the great international career that was to come.

The ambiance was strangely unglamorous. In this cold January, a flu epidemic had struck Munich, and one had to strain at times to hear the performance over the sneezing and coughing of the audience. During intermissions, the crowds promenaded in rank, as it were, along an oval pattern. There was an odd mixture of tuxedos, alpine mountain shoes, evening gowns and dirndls.

After the performance, my colleague, who had just sung Radames, his wife and I, had a bite at a local restaurant. The atmosphere reinforced the impression of gloom. After all the applause, there he sat, looking tired and lonely in this very quiet place, eating supper like any worker who just had finished a pedestrian day's work.

I flew on to Frankfurt and was driven over icy roads to Wiesbaden, my next audition spot. Here was a charming small spa in the French zone; it showed no war damage, had a delightful opera-theater-casino center, and altogether conveyed a much lighter, more pleasant atmosphere than the other cities I had visited. I was provided with an accompanist and rehearsal space for the audition, and was invited to that evening's performance of *The Marriage of Figaro*, a good, if not outstanding, performance.

The next day, I sang on the stage of the opera house for about thirty or more minutes. The current general manager, a stage director who had spent the war years as a refugee in Switzerland, invited me into his office. He asked many questions, and our conversation affected me deeply.

After he knew quite a bit about me, he told me that he would be delighted to offer me a contract. He believed that I had a lot of talent and voice; he also felt that he could teach me a lot and could provide me with an important artistic experience. Then, he shifted to an almost intimate, fraternal tone: "Do you really know what you are doing if you move from your newly found home in the United States to postwar Germany? Whatever you may view as limitations to your career there, you have a place you can belong to, and a climate in which you can move freely. Do you really want to exchange New York for a provincial city in occupied Germany? If I were given your choices, I would not budge away from what you have securely in the States, and I would not gamble on life here. Say the word, and I shall engage you, but think, think about it very carefully."

His words moved me deeply. I realized that he had addressed thoughts and emotions within me that I had not yet faced. I promised to weigh his advice thoroughly and was grateful for his interest.

That night, my last night in Europe, I went to the casino, only open to foreigners who had to show passports to be admitted. I threw my last few German marks on a seven on the roulette table, won, took my money and left. At the airport in Frankfurt, on my way back home, I bought a Leica camera with my winnings, and decided that, all things considered, it had been a worthwhile trip.

I had learned a lot and lived a lot in those last few days, and now I needed time to digest the experiences so that I could arrive at some closure. Had I not come to see for myself, I might have spent the rest of my life regretting the chances I had missed; now, I could draw on my own impressions to determine what future course my life should take.

How good it was to be back in New York. I needed to share the events of the last week with Marie who declared herself ready to go along with whatever path I might choose. As we pondered our future, it became clear to me that I did not want to live in Germany or Austria.

All moves in the pursuit of a career carry certain risks. My ambition was not powerful enough to overcome my distaste for the life I would encounter in Europe, even if I should be able to achieve the hoped-for success eventually. I was deeply concerned about how a move would affect my family; worse, I saw no way out once the choice was made to go. I knew that if we hated it there, we had no safety net. Without financial reserves we would be trapped with no way to return to the U.S. and start over. Again, we faced a situation when a few thousand dollars in reserve may have made a decisive difference. The risks were too frightening. But, beyond all realistic considerations, I believe my decision not to accept the engagements offered to me was based principally on emotional factors. It just didn't feel right.

XIII — AT THE CROSSROADS

The time for some serious thinking and planning had arrived. I was approaching my mid-thirties. Soon, I would no longer be able to hide behind the "young, promising singer" label. If my career as an opera and concert singer was to take off and provide a reasonable income and future, it had to happen pretty soon or never. I was feeling the strain of trying so hard and I needed to question, rigorously, what I could do and what I wanted to do.

With Europe out of the picture, the only hope for the kind of success in opera that would provide a decent livelihood was an engagement at the Metropolitan Opera in New York. I had done singing bits, and even a concert there, but that did not count in terms of becoming a full member of the company.

An audition on the stage of that venerable house, then on Thirty-Ninth Street and Seventh Avenue, was arranged so that Rudolf Bing, the General Manager, together with the leading conductors and artistic managers, could evaluate my suitability and chances. They would have to judge whether my voice was large enough to fill that huge space, whether there was enough quality and promise to engage me, and, if all other things were acceptable, whether there was an open spot in the current schedule of the Metropolitan for my voice and repertoire.

I was terror-stricken. I paced up and down backstage as I waited my turn. I was scheduled to go on after two internationally known singers had completed their auditions for specific parts.

Unlike my state of mind before the European auditions, I felt nearly paralyzed by stage fright. My mouth was dry, my heart pounded wildly, my feet felt weighed down as if by shoes of lead, I felt a powerful urge to run to the bathroom. Although I had lots of experience with stage jitters before performances and auditions, nothing compared to this. My body seemed to have divined that I was approaching a time of fateful decision and was reacting without consulting my brain.

Finally, I walked on stage. I faced the cavernous darkness of the huge, famous golden horseshoe auditorium and heard a disembodied voice ask me to choose my first aria. As I began with the Count's aria from the *Marriage of Figaro*, I felt myself calm down from panic to mere terror. The voice asked for two more selections from my repertoire as I steadied a bit. Then: "Thank you!" and my audition was over.

My manager who had been in the audience, had no word for me; I proceeded home with a colossal let down feeling. For the next four weeks I moved between anxiety and depression while I waited and received no response from the Met. The more time passed, the more I realized that in the words of the *Meistersinger's* immortal Beckmesser I had "versungen und vertan." I had failed to get an offer.

As the impact of this failure sank in, the forces of restitution in me, which had served me well in the past, began to go into high gear. Sometimes frantically, at other times more calmly, I started to consider my alternatives. Even though my mind was far from made up, I initiated steps to have my academic credits evaluated by the State Department of Education in Albany; this would give me some notion of where I would have to start should I decide to return to school. I also began some exploration of possible training opportunities in clinical psychology or medicine around the New York Metropolitan area.

It took another set of events to give me the final and decisive push that propelled me far away from my hopes of the last sixteen years. I had come full circle and was headed back to where I had started from. Perhaps I had really wanted to be there all along.

Columbia Masterworks was interested in having me record a longplaying disk of Viennese songs. With the help of Leo Taubman, who had accompanied my Town Hall debut, and Franz Mittler, a well-known Viennese pianist, arranger and composer, a group of outstanding Viennese musicians was assembled. Mittler arranged about ninety minutes of Viennese "Heurigen" songs and melodies for two pianos, violins, zither and baritone voice. Many of the pieces were classic Viennese folk tunes familiar to anyone growing up in Vienna. Some came from operettas, and classic "Singspiele," but most were from music performed in the winegardens, the "Heurigen," high in the Vienna Woods where recently harvested wines were served.

While these compositions did not necessarily represent great artistic genius, they were charming, easily singable, a bit senti-mental and sugary, yet easy to enjoy. They dealt with wine, love, youth, death, and again wine as the ultimate consoler. They faith-fully reflected the easygoing mood of the Heuriger where the aristocracy, middle class and servants drank their wine together and joined in these songs while looking on the city of Vienna below.

Recently, these melodies had become very popular in the States. Songs like "Vienna, City of My Dreams," and others of the same genre were being heard on the radio and in films. The musicians with me were, as I was, thoroughly imbued with the authentic style and manner of this music.

Felix Galimir of the Galimir Quartet was one of the violinists, the zither player had played for the hit film, *The Third Man* which took place in Vienna. The arrangements mixed instrumental marches and waltzes with about twenty songs. We had huge fun preparing for the recording sessions.

The project was titled "Dreams of Old Vienna," and my contract looked spectacularly detailed and impressive. I was to be paid the union minimum, something around $150 at the time of the actual recording; royalties on each record sold would be remitted to me every six months forever after.

This was another chance to have my career take off. Should the record become a success, I would not only be handsomely paid, but my reputation as a singer would ensure further engagements and popularity.

Columbia provided us with their finest studio, a converted church on Third Avenue in New York, with the latest in technical equipment; they appointed their top producer of classical records and their top engineer to handle the sessions. For three full days we recorded there until everyone who participated, including me, declared themselves satisfied with the final product. Whenever the producer had wanted another "take," all eyes in the studio were on Felix Galimir. He, the musicians' classic musician, always could be counted on to grit his teeth and grimace when he had to repeat a particularly "schmaltzy" passage and the rest of us waited for his expression to change.

I was roundly complimented by one and all, including those friends who heard the sample recording that I was given. I was pleased and full of hope.

Six months later, nothing had happened. A year later, urgent inquiries revealed startling information to me. Apparently, Columbia released only a small percentage of the records they cut. A board of merchandising experts determined whether the market was ready for a particular recording, and if they decided that a current release would not be timely, they just wrote the production expenses off as a loss. They liked my record, but decided not to release it. For the next five or so years I received a long accounting statement showing that as zero records had been sold, I was paid zero royalties. Hardly a surprise, as the record had never been released.

My disappointment and frustration delivered the final blow to my "artistic" goals. With renewed energy, I undertook Plan B. Back to School!

XIV — LIFE BEGINS AT THIRTY FIVE

The New York State Education Department had evaluated my academic credits; in effect, I was granted the equivalent of a Bachelor's Degree less twelve credit points. I needed to decide whether to put my energies into efforts to be admitted to a medical school or, as an alternative, to work towards a doctorate in clinical psychology.

I knew my general aspiration was to work with people in a helping capacity. As I grew older, my interests had shifted from the physical, the body, towards an understanding of people, myself, behavior, the human mind. I had to consider my need to support my family and myself; the rigid time requirements of a medical internship and residency would exclude even the limited time my cantorial work demanded. Clinical psychology promised more flexibility. I made my choice.

I applied for and took the Graduate Record Exam in Psychology, did reasonably well, and now began to make the rounds of the chairpersons who headed the various Clinical Psychology Programs at the local universities. To my shock and surprise–I had been used to the Viennese system which guaranteed admission if preliminary requirements had been met–I discovered that only about eight of four hundred qualified applicants to any of the Clinical Psychology Departments would be admitted to a doctoral program.

With nothing to lose, in a spirit of curious exploration, I started at the top, with the University I wanted most to attend, the one I considered most prestigious: Columbia. My interview with Professor Schaffer, the chairman, was very encouraging. He asked searching questions about my background in psychology which, in fact, did not exist, with the exception of one course in my last year of the Gymnasium. Surprisingly, he was familiar with the course content and quizzed me about it. Eventually, he voiced interest in my background, which was quite different from that of most other applicants, and which could agree with his philosophy of having students of diverse past experiences in the doctoral program. He suggested that I take some preliminary courses in clinical and experimental psychology and sociology. That would complete the twelve credits I needed, and, should I do well, he promised he would recommend my acceptance to the admissions committee.

I felt like dancing in the streets on my way home. My new approach to my life was underway. At the beginning of the next semester, I enrolled as an unmatriculated student in the courses Professor Schaffer had recommended, including one he taught himself on the "Psychology of Adjustment." It seemed a very new experience to sit in a classroom, study, take exams, write papers, and spend time in the library. Although difficult at first, I was highly motivated and truly fascinated by the material I was absorbing.

I sensed that I was on the road to making a dream come true that had been with me for as long as I could remember. Introspection, attempts to understand myself, my motivations and those of others, had been with me all along. I enjoyed meeting people and getting to know them. Almost intuitively, I had reached out to see beneath the surface of actions, to grasp what "made people tick." Some of that was reinforced in my acting training.

Several directors I had worked with emphasized the need for the actor to "feel" oneself into the character. They thought it important that the actor's walk, posture and manners reflect the personality and era of the role. That made it essential that the drama's character had to be "understood," that as much as possible had to be known about him or her; not only the obvious, but also about an emotional past which might have to be constructed if not enough was known.

These constructs came easily to me. I hoped that the training I was receiving would provide the tools to deepen my understanding of others, especially, of course, of my patients. I also felt that psychoanalytic training would offer the best foundation and that eventually the practice of psychotherapy would be most fulfilling for me.

In fact, my acting background proved very helpful in developing empathy so vital to the therapy process. The actor learns to form a stage personality from the details of the script. The analyst encounters a fully formed person and, together with the patient, works to uncover the details of background that may have led to the issues which brought the patient into treatment. The ability to enact emotionally the personality facing you, I knew, would be helpful to the understanding, not only intellectually, of the problems and conflicts that had to be confronted.

I had some problems with the behavioristic tradition at Columbia which required extensive work with conditioning and "rat psychology" experiments. It seemed quite a jump from counting animals pressing a bar to human behavior. Apparently such exposure was necessary to help acquire discipline in scientific method. Meaningful statistics could be more easily achieved with simple countable bits of animal behavior than with the complexity of the human beings in whom I was truly interested. Who was I to argue? I worked hard and ended up with "A"s in all three courses.

In a Social Psychology paper, I made my last concession to my former life. I completed a project that attempted to establish whether there was a relationship between high scores on a scale measuring "snobbery," and the preference of operagoers for hearing opera in the original language rather than in English translation. It was fun working on the research and interviewing the people who filled out my questionnaires. When it was all completed, I sent a copy to the music editor of the *New York Times* who mentioned it in the Sunday music section, leading to several "letters to the editor."

Columbia admitted me to graduate school, and in the following semester I was matriculated as a doctoral candidate in Clinical Psychology. The die was cast.

Everything now began to feel different. I continued my Cantorial work at the temple and accepted all possible singing engagements that fit into my study schedule. Those included performances with the New York City Opera where I sang the

Father in *Hänsel and Gretl* as well as Ochs in *Rosenkavalier*. But, the pressure was off. No longer was so much of my thinking and feeling overshadowed by a preoccupation with where my career was going and with what the future might hold for me. I was now directed to what seemed a clear road before me and, with new confidence, I never doubted that I would follow it.

Our environment began to change. We worked and socialized with people whose lifestyle and main interests were quite different from those of our friends who were performers, managers, and in other areas of show business; or for that matter, from the people in my congregation. The academicians of the faculty, the fellow students, the somewhat detached research people; the patients I began to work with as my internship started, the clinical supervisors, all seemed a very different crowd that presented new challenges and rewards.

Marie, who helped by working at a music school, related well to our new friends and acquaintances. There were quite a few parties and it took some time to make the transition from the outgoing, "always on" performers we had been accustomed to, to the more reserved, often shy, quiet, and somewhat introverted "scholars."

In addition to the course work and an original experimental dissertation, my doctorate required an approved clinical internship either for a full-time year or for three years part time. I chose the three part-time years with the Veterans Administration, which enabled me to continue supporting myself as I was paid a small salary as a civil service employee. Most attractive was that I could rotate after one year at a Psychiatric Hospital, to another year at a General Hospital and then for a third year to an outpatient clinic. Also, I was permitted and encouraged to pursue my dissertation research while interning.

It was one of the quirks of life that I received several major engagement offers on Broadway during my first three days of internship. A replacement was needed for a lead in *Fanny*, and I even went to meet the famous David Merrick, the producer who wanted to hear me. The telephone rang several times, with agents telling Marie: "Boy, do I have a job for your husband!" I felt a tiny twinge of temptation, but, it was easily resisted and outweighed by the totally irrational complaint: "Where were you when we needed you?"

My first year of internship was a real test of endurance. The hospital was in Lyons, New Jersey, forty miles from home, and I reported at eight in the morning. At eight-thirty, I led a group of schizophrenic patients who had been hospitalized for more than ten years and who were heavily dosed with Thorazine; it was not easy to keep them awake, to get them to interact, or to stay awake myself. My first diagnostic testing experience came when I was locked in a small room with a paranoid patient who weighed 300 pounds and was six feet, seven inches tall. I was told to administer projective tests, and so I did. I was too ignorant to be afraid.

After I arrived back home at six in the evening, I gulped down some food and went up to Columbia to attend my classes. Fridays, I drove straight to the Temple and sang services. For a year this went on through snow, ice or heat. On the two days that I was not at the hospital, I had a chance to study and attend additional classes. There were times when I confessed to Marie and to myself that, had I known what I had let myself in for, I might have reconsidered the whole idea.

But, my identity was changing. Even before I entered my own training analysis, my awareness of myself had increased. I recognized the difference between the performer and the healer. For a graduation of nurses at the hospital, I was asked to sing a solo. I cherish the printed program that announces: Vocal Solo, Manfred Hecht, **PSYCHOLOGIST**.

The last major hurdle, and it was major, was the dissertation. The woods were full of doctoral students who had finished all other requirements many years before, but never managed to complete their thesis and get their doctoral degree. I was determined that this would not happen to me. I was in a hurry to get on with it. In the second year of graduate school, with the help and support of the faculty I began to give serious thought to the selection of my project.

Eventually, I developed the outline of a study of "Perception of Parental Figures in Schizophrenia," had it approved, and embarked on what was probably the most arduous, strenuous, anxiety-ridden and frustrating research as well as period of my life. I collected data by running thirty schizophrenic patients, and thirty so-called "normal" subjects through a series of tests, including the showing of a twenty minute motion picture. In addition, I tested a "cross validation sample" of ninety men.

The effort it took to recruit subjects, process them, perform the appropriate statistical procedures and write up a meaningful and acceptable scientific paper was enormous. The results of my research were negative, meaning that my data did not support certain theoretical notions that had been proposed in the literature, and which I was testing experimentally. I had to undertake a series of complicated calculations (before the days of easily available computers) to prove that my data were reliable, and that they indeed measured what they were supposed to measure.

Miraculously, I survived with the generous help of my faculty committee. On a warm afternoon in April 1958, I appeared before a group of professors who were experts in the area of my research to defend my dissertation. As I droned on with my presentation, I hoped fervently that I might put them to sleep before their questioning began. They did, however, question me rigorously, and, after I was asked to wait outside for a short while, they called me back and greeted me as a newly created Ph.D. I now was Doctor Hecht, the last four years had achieved what I hoped they would, and amidst the turmoil of emotions that swept through me, I realized that I now was ready to file the traditionally required copy of my dissertation at the Library of Congress.

Amidst the joy, pride and relief I felt, I must admit to a sense of saturation with experimental research. Perhaps, unfortunately, my appetite for further such studies seemed stilled for good.

What I wanted most when I chose Clinical Psychology, was to acquire the necessary skills to work clinically and therapeutically with people. Knowledge and experience in research and diagnostic testing gave me the necessary background to what I really aimed for, namely, psychotherapy.

My doctorate provided a base; I knew it did not prepare me adequately for individual practice. To qualify properly, I felt I needed extensive post-doctoral training. That, in my opinion, could only be provided by an accredited psychoanalytic institute.

As long as I could remember, I had been fascinated by psychoanalysis. I was convinced that, while it was still evolving, psychoanalytic theory presented the most comprehensive model of human behavior and I was eager to learn all I could about it.

At that time only two psychoanalytic institutes trained non-medical candidates. The Postgraduate Center for Mental Health, my first choice, had accepted me after a lengthy and complicated screening procedure, provided I received my doctorate in the spring of 1958. My second phone call, after informing Marie that I had passed my orals, was to their registrar who confirmed my acceptance and welcomed me to the Institute. The path to the next level of my new career was open and waiting for me. I wished I could tell my parents.

Before me lay five years of analytic training, my own psychoanalysis, the challenge of opening my own private practice, and all the familiar steps of striving for success. This time it was not for engagements and reviews, but above all for personal growth, learning and maturing. Eventually, of course, for the scale of appointments that were the backbone of a professional career: psychoanalytic certification, supervisory and consultants' appointments, teaching positions, academic and/or administrative appointments. I needed to establish myself and to rise in the hierarchy of the profession.

This reaching was different from the efforts of previous years. I now had acquired the bona fide credentials and skills that qualified me as a professional. I hoped I was earning the respect and the acknowledgment of my peers and mentors. Perhaps that had been true for my aspirations as a performer as well. But, once licensed, there were now ample opportunities to practice my skills.

In opera and concert there was that tiny space at the top of the pyramid reserved for the superstars who could achieve fame and support themselves with some dignity. There was mighty little below that. Every audition, every performance, was a trial to prove that one belonged up there.

As psychologist, psychoanalyst, therapist, I could do my work, even if I had a cold or a bad stomach. Were I to make an error, I would have a chance to correct it without having to fear that dozens were waiting in the wings to replace me. I was gaining that sense of stability for which I had yearned. Beyond all the other gratifications I found in my work, I was now offered a chance to earn a reasonably comfortable, steady income. In the light of my past experiences, I was in dire need of such consistent reassurance. From that base I could concentrate my energies on my work, build on and love what I was doing without the constant gnawing fear of imminent failure.

The next few years presented a life entirely different from the past. My own analysis, the intense experiences and the learning that are part of the practice of psychoanalysis and psychotherapy could fill another book. Some of it was funny, some of it tragic, much of it anxiety-charged to a greater or lesser degree, almost nothing boring.

I shall not soon forget one of my earliest patients, a man with a background of long jail terms for violent crimes, saying to me: "Doc, what I tell you dies with you?!" Or the airline attendant, a mirror image of Marilyn Monroe, telling me in her first session: "Gee, it's so much easier for me to talk after I have been to bed with someone. What's the couch here for?" Or the attractive woman patient who walked in for her session in a fur coat, opened her coat, revealed a nude body and proclaimed: "When I told you the other day that I was ugly, you didn't agree!"

XV — WHO AM I?

With my doctorate, license, and analytic certification I had acquired another of the varied identities that my life had presented me with. From the little Jewish boy, growing up in the fairly privileged middle-class family environment of Vienna, I had gone on to be a music student, then a medical student. After a period of being hunted for what I was, I became a refugee in a foreign land and endeavored with all my might to become an "American." I succeeded to some extent in feeling that I belonged, that I was in my heart and soul an "American." I managed to survive, and to establish some prospects for a possible life as singer and performer. There were the Broadway shows and the beginning buds of a career in concert and opera. Also, I became a husband, and took the place of a father.

Then, I was a soldier. For two and a half years, my life was not only dominated by the now familiar urge to survive, but also by the necessity to see the evils of Hitler's conquest undone, and, most important, to try and save my parents.

After failing at that, efforts resumed to build a life as a struggling singer and performer. While survival, at least in financial terms was, at times precarious, somehow I muddled through and it began to look as if I may yet succeed in establishing a consistent path to a "career" in concert and opera.

On the way, a new identity came along. I became, in popular perception, a member of the clergy. In spite of some difficulties of accepting myself in the clerical role of "Cantor," I apparently succeeded in ways satisfactory to my congregation and to me as the person who led them in musical prayer. This new me happened unexpectedly and suddenly, but I was able to adapt to it without feeling or being hypocritical. I came to appreciate what I was doing, and was grateful for the support this role gave me.

Finally, another, very different, me emerged. As I took my turn back to school on my way to becoming a psychologist, I came very close to where I had expected to be many years before, when I had been delighted to be a medical student until cruel forces beyond my control had redirected my entire life.

Throughout, I was ruled by the need to survive, hopeful that I could do so without being ruthless or unethical. I had to compromise; at times, I followed paths that I was not especially proud of, yet I never knowingly did anything that caused me shame. Without consciously even realizing it, I tried to be true to Hillel's principle: "If I am not for myself, who will be; if I am all for myself, who am I?"

As I review some of the high points of my life, I am left with many questions and few answers. Is there a thread that connects the various phases I experienced? Can I ever understand the forces that brought me to the present? Did I make the "right" choices? What would my life be now, had I chosen differently? Where do I truly fit in? How do the elements of Vienna, Jewishness, America, Music, Psychology, and all the other diverse aspects of my experiences meet?

The answers will never be fully available. Perhaps, this is as it should be; perhaps, there is no need to search for what can never be fully discovered; perhaps, it is better to accept what is and to attempt to make the best of the opportunities that remain.

A passage from Ecclesiastes (3:19-22) comes to mind which Brahms has set to music in the first of his Four Serious Songs. Freely translated, it reads:

"Therefore I saw that there is nothing of greater worth than that man be happy in his work, for that is his lot."